Ethics in
Public Relations

D0161041

Ethics in Public Relations

A Guide to Best Practice

Second Edition

Patricia J Parsons

CHARTERED INSTITUTE OF PUBLIC RELATIONS

KOGAN
PAGE

London and Philadelphia

Publisher's note

Every possible effort has been made to ensure that the information contained in this book is accurate at the time of going to press, and the publishers and author cannot accept responsibility for any errors or omissions, however caused. No responsibility for loss or damage occasioned to any person acting, or refraining from action, as a result of the material in this publication can be accepted by the editor, the publisher or the author.

First published in Great Britain and the United States in 2004 by Kogan Page Limited
Reprinted 2005, 2007
Second edition 2008

120 Pentonville Road
London N1 9JN
United Kingdom
www.koganpage.com

525 South 4th Street, #241
Philadelphia PA 19147
USA

ISBN   978 0 7494 5332 9

British Library Cataloguing-in-Publication Data

A CIP record for this book is available from the British Library.

Library of Congress Cataloging-in-Publication Data

Parsons, Patricia (Patricia Houlihan)
   Ethics in public relations : a guide to best practice / Patricia J. Parsons. -- 2nd ed.
      p. cm.
   Includes index.
   ISBN 978-0-7494-5332-9
   1. Public relations--Moral and ethical aspects. 2. Public relations--Management. I. Title
   HD59.P3548 2008
   174'.96592--dc22

                                                                2008025633

Typeset by Jean Cussons Typesetting, Diss, Norfolk
Printed and bound in India by Replika Press Pvt Ltd

Contents

Contents

List of figures

PR in Practice Series

Published in association with the Chartered Institute of Public Relations
Series Editor: Anne Gregory

Kogan Page has joined forces with the Chartered Institute of Public Relations to publish this unique series, which is designed specifically to meet the needs of the increasing numbers of people seeking to enter the public relations profession and the large band of existing PR professionals. Taking a practical, action-oriented approach, the books in the series concentrate on the day-to-day issues of public relations practice and management rather than academic history. They provide ideal primers for all those on CIPR, CAM and CIM courses or those taking NVQs in PR. For PR practitioners, they provide useful refreshers and ensure that their knowledge and skills are kept up to date.

Professor Anne Gregory is one of the UK's leading public relations academics. She is Pro Vice Chancellor of Leeds Metropolitan University and Director of the Centre for Public Relations Studies in the Business School. She is the UK's only full-time professor of public relations. Before becoming an academic, Anne spent 12 years in public relations practice and has experience at a senior level both in-house and in consultancy. She remains involved in consultancy work, having clients in both the public and private sectors, and is a non-executive director of South West Yorkshire Mental Health NHS Trust with special responsibility for financial and communication issues. Anne is Consultant Editor of the PR in Practice series and edited the book of the same name and wrote *Planning and Managing Public Relations Campaigns*, also in this series. She was President of the CIPR in 2004.

Other titles in the series:

Creativity in Public Relations by Andy Green
Effective Internal Communication by Lyn Smith and Pamela Mounter
Effective Media Relations by Michael Bland, Alison Theaker and David Wragg
Effective Writing Skills for Public Relations by John Foster
Managing Activism by Denise Deegan
Online Public Relations by David Phillips
Planning and Managing Public Relations Campaigns by Anne Gregory
Public Affairs in Practice by Stuart Thompson and Steve John
Public Relations: A practical guide to the basics by Philip Henslowe
Public Relations in Practice edited by Anne Gregory
Public Relations Strategy by Sandra Oliver
Risk Issues and Crisis Management in Public Relations by Michael Regester and Judy Larkin
Running a Public Relations Department by Mike Beard

The above titles are available from all good bookshops. To obtain further information, please go to the CIPR website (www.cipr.co.uk/books) or contact the publishers at the address below:

Kogan Page Ltd
120 Pentonville Road
London N1 9JN
Tel: 020 7278 0433   Fax: 020 7837 6348
www.koganpage.com

About the author

Patricia J Parsons is Professor of Public Relations at Mount Saint Vincent University in Halifax, Nova Scotia, Canada. A past-chair of the Department of Public Relations, she teaches ethics and strategic public relations planning in both the undergraduate and graduate degree programmes. Her academic research and writing have been primarily in the areas of public relations ethics and strategy, and healthcare communication. She is accredited in public relations by the Canadian Public Relations Society and was admitted to the CPRS College of Fellows in 2005.

About the consultant editor

Professor Anne Gregory, FCIPR, is Director of the Centre for Public Relations at Leeds Metropolitan University and the UK's only full-time Professor of Public Relations. Originally a broadcast journalist, Anne spent 10 years in public relations practice at senior levels both in-house and in consultancy before moving on to an academic career. Anne was President of the Chartered Institute of Public Relations in 2004. She initiated and edits the CIPR's *Public Relations in Practice* series of books and is managing editor of the *Journal of Communication Management*.

Anne is actively involved in PR practice, being a non-Executive Director of South West Yorkshire NHS Mental Health Trust with special responsibility for finance and communication. She is also a practising public relations consultant and trainer.

Foreword

If there is one question that haunts the public relations industry it's the question of ethics.

In recent years there has been increasing alarm about 'spin', particularly in the political and business environments, and this has had a knock-on effect on the public relations industry as a whole. It is ironic that at the very time when professional communicators are being used more and more and their expertise is being recognized, there are also persistent rumblings about the integrity of the practice.

We can all think of defining moments when the ethics of the profession have been questioned, but it's also true to say that the vast majority of practitioners do their job with honesty and openness, trying to be fair both to the organization they represent and to those who they are dealing with in the external world.

However, there is no doubt that public relations people sometimes face difficulties in the complex working environment in which they operate. Although they want to tell the truth, sometimes their understanding of the truth is imperfect for a variety of reasons. Making consistent ethical decisions in a diverse world where cultures and values clash is not easy. Being loyal to employers while living with conscience can bring conflict.

That's where *Ethics in Public Relations* by Patricia Parsons can help. Not many public relations people have had training in ethics and ethical decision-making and this book fills that gap. In a very readable and logical manner the author takes us through the practical world of ethics, dealing with definitions, some basic ethical theories and principles and some typical ethical problems. She then goes on to talk about ethics and the practitioner, getting personal. She asks the reader to examine their own moral principles and how these underpin approaches to practice. Looking then at current public relations practice, the author presents us with some of the real ethical challenges that confront those involved, outlining some ethical decision-making tools that can be used to ensure that a thoughtful and consistent approach is taken. She rounds off with some reflections about accountable public relations, drawing out the implications for practice as a whole.

All those practitioners who belong to professional bodies sign up to a code of conduct. Indeed, the Global Alliance of Public Relations and Communication Management thought that ethics was so important that agreeing a global ethical protocol was its first major project when it was formed in 2001. However, codes and protocols need translating into reality. Patricia Parson's book will help busy practitioners who are concerned about ethics to do just that.

Professor Anne Gregory
Consultant Editor

Preface

Fourteen years ago, I began teaching a course in organizational public relations to second-year public relations students in our four-year undergraduate degree programme. At the time, the curriculum required a section on ethics. To my colleagues in the department, I appeared to be the most likely candidate to teach this since my background was in medical communications and I had already co-authored two books – one a textbook and one a trade book – on healthcare ethics. Surely this would be a natural progression for me. To some extent they were right.

I began doing background research on the 'field' of public relations ethics. The 'field' was small to say the least. Whereas there was much material in the academic journals as well as in industry publications about the *status* of ethics and ethical behaviour and what ought to be done in both the academic discipline (we ought to be teaching it) and the practice of public relations (we ought to be more ethical), there was really very little that was useful for either neophyte or seasoned practitioners in their daily practice. As a budding academic, I jumped into the fray and began some academic publishing to contribute to the theoretical basis. This, however, did not help much in trying to find practical materials for helping both students and practitioners to understand the ethical issues inherent in our field, nor did it help them to clarify their own principles and values in making ethically defensible decisions.

This book is the result of this search for more practically useful materials and is my contribution to helping public relations practitioners understand when they are faced with ethical dilemmas and how to think about their actions and the consequences. Indeed, it is directed towards public relations practitioners and all those interested in public communication who seek an examination of the practical applications of ethical thinking. But, perhaps even more important, this book is for those who would not normally read a book about ethics. It has been my experience that those who avoid ethics books do so often because the material that they have been exposed to in the past seemed so far away from their real worlds. I hope that this book will bring ethics closer to that everyday reality. The fact that a non-academic approach to ethics in our professional discipline is even in your hands is a testimony to the forward thinking on the part of the Chartered Institute of Public Relations in the United Kingdom.

The purpose of *Ethics in Public Relations: A Guide to Best Practice* is three-fold:

- to provide you with a framework for understanding important ethical issues in the field of public relations and corporate communications today and in the future;
- to help you to develop an attitude that supports the concept that ethics is key to professionalism and credibility in the field; and
- to assist you in your everyday ethical decision-making.

The aim of this book is not to provide another tome on the philosophical ethical theory that is so prevalent in many business ethics books today (and which students at the undergraduate level seem to be singularly averse to), rather to relate underlying theories directly to everyday issues. I hope that you will appreciate the distinctly non-academic style of this book which I think is so important to get you to think about your personal and professional value systems so that you can do some real soul-searching. I believe that taking a long, hard look at ourselves is where ethical thought really begins, but it does highlight an important question: Can you really *learn* ethics?

Any professor who believes that his or her book or course on ethics will ensure ethics in practice is living in a dream world. I believe that all we can reasonably hope to accomplish is to make students and practitioners alike think about the issues and perhaps see situations in more than a black and white way. Ethics in this book is akin to drawing a black line through a grey area. You are as comfortable as possible with where you draw the black line, but the situation may still be grey. However, by the time you reach the final chapter of this book, I believe that you may have a better answer, at least for yourself, to the question about whether or not ethics can be learnt.

To get you to that point, the book is divided into four parts. In the first part, we'll examine together some of the underlying considerations and principles that generally guide ethical thinking. Part 2 focuses on you; how your own sense of morality developed and how you use that in situations that have a direct, personal impact on you. The third part places under an ethical microscope some of the strategies and tactics that are widely used in public relations today. Finally, we take a broader perspective by looking at the role public relations plays in the ethics of organizations in general and the future of our field.

I would be very interested in how this book might have helped you in your study and practice of public relations in the 21st century. Please let me know.

Part 1

What lies beneath

Recognizing, facing and dealing with ethical dilemmas in our everyday practice of public relations and corporate communications are the three most important aspects of the realities of ethics. Underneath this surface, however, are fundamental concerns about definitions (can we come to a consensus?), principles (what are the most important values in public relations?) and even some theory (how would the philosophers have viewed some of our issues?) that can be truly useful in practice.

The chapters that follow are devoted to setting up an ethical framework by examining ethical theory with an eye to practical applications. We can hardly discuss the everyday practice if we don't come to some consensus on definitions of such terms as ethics, professionalism and the truth. In addition, issues such as rights and rules need some discussion so that we can move on to looking at you, the practitioner, and the ethical dilemmas inherent in the work you do.

1

Before we begin: new profession... or one of the oldest?

The cosmos is neither moral nor immoral; only people are.
He who would move the world must first move himself.

Edward Ericson

It's September. The air is filled with anticipation on the university campus. I watch the new students eagerly file into a classroom of higher learning, every one of them with a slightly different belief about their chosen field of study – public relations – a hard one to explain to family and friends. And most have the often misguided impression that what they need most to be successful in this field is to be a so-called 'people person'.

I move quickly to disabuse them of this notion. I tell them that if they are people persons, then perhaps they are most suited to working as one of the helping professionals – be a physician, a nurse, a massage therapist, I tell them, but PR may not be what you think it is. I tell them that in this field of public relations they'll be spending a lot more time relating to their computers and their deadlines, especially in the early years of their careers. Then I ask these neophyte public relations practitioners to rate a series of personal characteristics according to how important they believe each one is in the successful practice of public relations. On the list are such qualities as intelligence, flexibility, personality, maturity, creativity, sophistication, courage and integrity.

I gather the papers to tabulate their responses and note that these rarely vary from year to year. With few exceptions, integrity rates on the lower end of the scale of importance, often dead last. Does this mean that we can expect public relations practitioners of the future to have the moral scruples of Attila the Hun? Or does it mean that in the grand scheme of things, they have not given much conscious thought to how personal integrity and character fit into their dream job? Maybe they do not truly understand the meaning of the word integrity. Perhaps they're a bit like you.

So, how do you rate in the integrity department? Have you ever written and issued a news release that was less than truthful – misleading, perhaps? Would you do it if your boss asked you to do so? Have you ever tried to bribe a reporter? Or would you? (It wasn't really a bribe, you say, just a small token.) Are you even aware when you cross the line? Do you have the personal tools for solving these everyday moral dilemmas you face?

There is little doubt that our publics – including employees, the media, our clients and consumers, to name but a few – are already highly sceptical of what is communicated to them on a daily basis. We can't really afford to contribute any more to this mistrust, which leads us to the question: just how important *is* ethics in PR?

You may remember Ivy Lee as the so-called father of modern public relations. But you are probably less familiar with his partner Tommy Ross. I can no longer recall where I read it but he is reported to have said 'Unless you are willing to resign an account or a job over a matter of principle, it is no use to call yourself a member of the world's newest profession – you're already a member of the world's oldest.' Ouch, that hurts.

PUBLIC RELATIONS ETHICS: OXYMORON?

More than one public relations practitioner has had to defend the occupation when confronted by a hostile sceptic suggesting that 'public relations ethics' is an oxymoron. Indeed, critics can provide us with chapter and verse on the more unsavoury aspects of this advocacy field. Consider media critic Joyce Nelson's 1989 description of public relations in her book *Sultans of Sleaze: Public relations and the media*: 'The power of the PR industry is demonstrated by its... remarkable ability to function as a virtually invisible "grey eminence" behind the scenes, gliding in and out of troubled situations with the ease of a Cardinal Richelieu and the con-science of a mercenary.'[1] And it is clear that she is not alone in her view.

There is little doubt that, even today, public relations as an industry still suffers from a bad reputation. Consider journalism professor Stuart Ewen's 1996 book *PR! A Social History of Spin*, where he describes what he calls a 'foundational conceit' in the field of public relations – conceit born of the notion that the public mind can and should be manipulated. In addition, media watchers John Stauber and Sheldon Rampton continue to provide a running commentary on the unsavory aspects of public rela-tions as they see them, as chronicled on their sweeping *PR Watch* website http://www.prwatch.com, and in their books *Toxic Sludge is Good for You!: The public relations industry unspun; Trust Us, We're Experts! How industry manipulates science and gambles with your future* and *The Best War Ever: Lies, damned lies and the mess in Iraq*.

Perhaps we need to take a more careful look at how the public may have come to the conclusion that our chosen field of practice and study has the moral character of a con man.

A TARNISHED HISTORY

There's a Yiddish proverb that goes like this: 'A half-truth is a whole lie.' Whereas much of the history of public relations might not be peppered with in-your-face lies, one could make the case that half-truths are rampant. There is little doubt that the public's image of public relations is less than spotless. Indeed, the media tend to lead the public to believe that there is something just a little, or sometimes a lot, dishonest about public relations. Half-truths or whole lies, is the public justified in this opinion?

American author and creator of the Ziggy cartoons Tom Wilson is reputed to have said 'Honesty is the best image', and that comment, perhaps more than any other, speaks to the need for integrity and veracity in public communication. It seems that there is a practical side to the notion of ethics in public communication. We are in the business of image-building for employers and clients, while at the same time building an image for our own field. Historically, honesty has not always been a part of that image.

Whenever anyone points out to us, the modern public relations practi-tioners, that P T Barnum represented much of what is dishonest in the history of this field, we're quick to point out that he was a 'publicist' who lived in a different era. No one could truly call him a member of the public relations 'profession' (more about that term later). Every professional discipline has evolved. But even throughout the 20th century when modern public relations practice was born, we continued to find ample fodder for the image that public relations is perhaps less than honest.

Modern public relations in the developed world today can arguably trace its roots to the United States of the early 20th century and people such as Edward Bernays and Ivy Lee. In his book *PR! A Social History of Spin*, social historian and media critic Stuart Ewen describes Bernays as 'a farsighted architect of modern propaganda techniques who, dramatically, from the early 1920s onward, helped to consolidate a fateful marriage between theories of mass psychology and schemes of corporate and political persuasion.'[2]

A nephew of Sigmund Freud, Bernays was convinced that a 'public relations counsellor' (a term he is reputed to have coined) should use social science approaches to manipulate the masses into thinking the way they ought to think, and the way they ought to think is the way the social elite thinks. In 1928, Bernays wrote in his book *Propaganda*, 'The conscious and intelligent manipulation of the organized habits and opinions of the masses is an important element in a democratic society... Those who manipulate this unseen mechanism... constitute an invisible government which is the true ruling power of our country.'[3] While you may not appreciate Bernays' remarks about manipulation and all that this connotes, his reference to the power of public relations cannot be ignored.

In the 1930s, public relations pioneer Carl Byoir is reputed to have invented the bogus grassroots campaign by setting up dummy organizations such as the National Consumers' Tax Organization to lobby against special taxes on chain stores, a tactic which was carried out at the behest of his client, grocery giant A & P.[4] Retrospectively, this kind of approach seems clearly dishonest to most PR practitioners. Yet a quick perusal of the PR Watch website[5] provides a running list of current front groups whose backers and funders are not always transparent – clearly Byoir's legacy. The organization PR Watch describes itself as one that helps the public 'recognize manipulative and misleading PR practices'. Their two main staff members are John Stauber and Sheldon Rampton, co-authors of two recent books mentioned above that take aim at dishonest and manipulative public relations tactics.

The power of public relations to shape opinions is one of the most compelling reasons to consider our duties to society and to take care not to abuse that power by the dishonest use of manipulation. But if you think that this kind of manipulative ploy is relegated to the historical roots of modern PR, then think again.

Consider, within recent memory, Hill and Knowlton's campaign to stimulate American public support for the first war against Iraq, for which the Kuwait government reputedly paid them US$10 million for the job.[6] A major part of their strategy involved the creation and distribution of a video news release featuring a young Kuwaiti woman's testimony before a congressional committee. The woman related a startling story of unspeakable Iraqi army atrocities, perhaps the most graphic of which was the story of babies being dumped from incubators in Kuwait hospitals. Identified only as Nayirah, the girl and her testimony was riveting and destined to achieve public support. Later, enterprising journalists who had not thought to ask about her identity earlier discovered that Nayirah was actually the daughter of the Kuwaiti ambassador, coached for her performance by her public relations handler and without any first-hand knowledge that any such atrocities had ever taken place. But, by the time this was discovered the damage was already done: opinions had been formed based on her testimony and action had been taken.

Wouldn't it be better if we just forgot about this stuff and went on with our jobs? After all, most public relations practitioners are involved in a wide variety of well-conceived, honest and ethical approaches to achieving mutual support and respect between their clients and their publics. Although this may be true, we all have to stand accountable for what the public sees as the sins of our profession. Indeed, public and media misunderstanding of our motives and objectives can impede our ability to do our work honestly and ethically.

As social trends of the past quarter-century have resulted in the need for more strategic communication between organizations and their publics, there has been a concomitant increasing focus on the ethical behaviour of those organizations. As the interface between the organization and its publics, and arguably the keeper of the organizational reputation, the public relations function has an even more important role as the social conscience of the organization. Someone has to provide guidance on organizational action for the purposes of considering the greater good. Public relations is particularly well situated to accomplish this. After all, we are the ones who are supposed to be tracking trends and issues in our economic, political and social environments so that we can propose ways that our clients and organizations can prevent problems and capitalize on emerging opportunities. While carrying out this environmental scanning role we have a distinct opportunity to uncover potential ethical transgressions and to recommend ways to avoid impropriety as well as the appearance of misbehaviour.

It seems clear that the public may be at least partly justified in their negative perception of PR. We can only change that image when every PR practitioner accepts personal and professional responsibility for his or her own actions, and values integrity above all.

DEFINING OUR TERMS

The term *ethics* falls off the tongue very easily these days, yet many people who use it have not taken the time to consider its true meaning.

7

In the late 1960s, former dean and president of Loyola University in Chicago Raymond Baumhart (who holds a doctorate in business administration as well as being a Jesuit priest), wrote the now-classic book *An Honest Profit: What businessmen say about ethics in business.*[7] He asked businessmen of the age what ethics meant to them, to which they gave a variety of responses from references to their feelings about what is right or wrong, through religious beliefs, to doing what the law requires. Some suggested that they did not, in fact, know what ethics really meant at all. Perhaps these were the honest ones.

An examination of what something is *not*, however, can sometimes be helpful in determining a useful definition of it.

First, ethics is not merely what has become accepted practice within the industry. Just because something wrong has been done over and over again through the years does not make it the right thing to do. Indeed, the history of human existence on this earth has been riddled with activities that were deemed acceptable – slavery, child labour and human sacrifice come immediately to mind. However, just because they were deemed permissible at a certain point in history does not necessarily make them morally acceptable for all times. For example, setting up front groups that hide their true agenda might have been accepted PR practice in the past; however, that does not mean that today's publics are prepared to accept them as morally appropriate.

Second, ethics is not merely a question of figuring out what you can get away with. Not getting caught doing something wrong does not make it right. Doing the right thing only to serve your own needs is often considered to be the hallmark of an individual who is functioning at a low level of moral development. In fact, our prisons are filled with people who thought it was all right to do something if they did not get caught. (We discuss moral development more fully in Chapter 7). Thus, from a practical standpoint, it might be time for organizations to consider that being ethical means considering the needs of others as well. Creating a PR campaign that considers only the needs of the organization without respect for the public's needs could today be construed as unethical.

Finally, ethics is more than simply following the letter of the law. It is a fallacy to assume that everything that is legal is also morally correct; it is equally problematic to presume that everything you consider to be ethical must therefore be legal. Law and morality are related, but they are certainly not the same thing. Organizations that follow the letter of the law and nothing more are clearly looking out for their own needs, without considering the possibility that their responsibility to their communities might be morally rather than simply legally dictated. What they *ought to do* might be considerably more than what they *must do*. Now that we have established what ethics is not, perhaps we're a step closer to what it is.

Philosophers define ethics as the study of moral rightness or wrongness, which is limited by the human ability to reason. Our decisions are only as good as our human reasoning abilities. Whereas philosophers have the luxury of simply studying these issues, as professionals we need to be able actually to apply aspects of philosophical rumination. Thus, we can think of 'public relations ethics' as...

> ... the application of knowledge, understanding and reasoning to questions of right or wrong behaviour in the professional practice of public relations.

We'll use this as our fundamental definition as we move through our discussions. In practical terms, someone once defined ethical decision-making as drawing a black line through that grey area I mentioned in the preface. The area will always remain grey but at some point each of us has to draw that line. As you will see, there are few clear-cut solutions to ethical dilemmas, but as a professional it is your responsibility to determine what might be the right place to draw that line.

A PROFESSION OR PROFESSIONALISM?

It is clear that the concept of professionalism is closely tied to ethics – professional ethics to be more precise. All you need to do is a quick search of websites on professionalism and you will rapidly come up with an extensive listing that is almost entirely sites with the words 'ethics and professionalism'. But what is this elusive notion of professionalism? How important is it? And, closest to home, how do you cultivate it?

Who cares if the public views public relations as a profession, an occupation, a vocation or just a job? Evidently, public relations associations do. According to the website of the Global Alliance for Public Relations and Communication Management (of which the Chartered Institute of Public Relations, the Canadian Public Relations Society and the Public Relations Society of America, among others, are members), a profession is distinguished by specific characteristics, including 'master of a particular intellectual skill through education and training, acceptance of duties to a broader society than merely one's clients/employers, objectivity [and] high standards of conduct and performance'.[8] It is this last tenet that places professional ethics squarely in the domain of defining a profession. And it seems clear that from a public relations perspective, it is in PR's best interest to be viewed by the public as a profession (rather than an occupation or a job). Whether or not this designation is of any material value doesn't seem to be on anyone's radar screen. That, however, is quite a separate argument. For now, it seems important to a lot of people within our field that it be seen as a profession. It is clearly a part of our image.

So, one might conclude, professionalism is something characteristic only of members of so-called professions. Where does that leave all those people whose occupations do not seem to display those characteristics of a profession? Can they not be deemed to have a high level of *professionalism*? Intuitively, I'm sure you know that they certainly can.

What about that waiter at your favourite restaurant whose *professionalism* shines through in the way he treats you and his other customers? What about your cleaning lady whose pride in the quality of her work always makes you think that she shows great professionalism? It is this quality of professionalism that sets individuals apart from their peers, even if they don't work in disciplines with high levels of education and training and codes of professional standards (ie ethics).

On the other hand, don't you know people who belong to traditional professions such as medicine, law and the clergy whose behaviour clearly indicates a lack of professionalism? One need only read the newspaper every day to see examples of such individuals.

ASPIRING TO PROFESSIONALISM

It seems that professionalism is at least partially about respecting other people as you go about your work, and respect is clearly an aspect of ethics. But professionalism is more than this. More than once, I've heard the opinion that professionalism, simply stated, means doing what is right. Is that not what integrity and the application of your ethical standards are all about? Of course it is. But it's more than that.

In his book *True Professionalism: The courage to care about your people, your clients, and your career*, writer David Maister suggests that…

> … professionalism is predominantly an attitude, not a set of competencies... real professionalism has little, if anything, to do with which business you are in, what role within that business you perform, or how many degrees you have. Rather it implies pride in work, a commitment to quality, a dedication to the interests of the client, and a sincere desire to help.[9]

It seems cultivating professionalism as a personal quality is one way you can move towards an ethical approach to your work in public relations.

MEASURING YOUR PROFESSIONALISM QUOTIENT

Based on what professionalism as a characteristic is perceived to be, you might consider your own level of professionalism. Figure 1.1 provides you with a brief test to get you started thinking about your own level of professionalism as it relates to your ethical standards.

Measuring your PQ*
(*Professionalism Quotient)

1. Do you always treat people you work with (including bosses, clients, people you manage) with the respect you expect to be afforded?
   a) always
   b) usually
   c) rarely
   d) never

2. Are you courteous in your communication (even on the phone and in e-mail) with others?
   a) always
   b) usually
   c) rarely
   d) never

3. Do you do every assigned task to the best of your ability?
   a) always
   b) usually
   c) rarely
   d) never, if I can get away with it

4. Do you do what you know to be right from a moral perspective?
   a) always try
   b) only when I think someone might be looking
   c) I do what is right for me
   d) I couldn't care less about doing the right thing

5. Do you keep up to date on what's going on in the field of public relations?
   a) Yes, I'm dedicated to continuing education both formally & informally
   b) I try to. I read the trade literature
   c) I read stuff when I get a chance
   d) Why should I? I know enough

Here's how to score yourself: Give yourself five points for every a, three for a b, one for a c and no points for a d.

25 points: You truly demonstrate professionalism. You would be a good role model for neophyte public relations practitioners. Most employers would be proud to have you on their staff.

21–24 points: You are not quite there. You probably consider yourself to be a professional, but you don't quite have what it takes to demonstrate what others would describe unconditionally as professionalism. Sometimes just being aware of your shortcomings can move you toward fixing them.

18–20 points: You need some professionalism intervention. It's time to re-examine your personal ethics and your work ethic, but there is probably hope.

Under 18 points: Are you aware that you might be contributing to public relations' less-than-spotless reputation?

Figure 1.1 *Measuring your PQ*

Obviously, this test is just for fun, but professionalism in public relations is a serious matter. Perhaps if we had a collection of people who clearly demonstrate professionalism, we wouldn't need to worry any longer about whether or not public relations is a profession. Professionalism is key to personal ethics.

Before we move on to a discussion of that sticky issue of 'the truth', perhaps you were wondering how we defined integrity in that first-year public relations class that I took you into at the beginning of this chapter. We determined it to be doing the right thing even when no one's looking. What's the right thing? That is what we are about to discover together.

Notes

1. Nelson, J (1989) *Sultans of Sleaze: Public relations and the media*, Between the Lines Press, Toronto, p 19
2. Ewen, S (1996) *PR! A Social History of Spin*, Basic Books, New York, p 3
3. Bernays, E (1928) *Propaganda*, Kennikat Press, New York
4. Bleifuss, J (1994) Flack attack, *Utne Reader*, January–February, pp 72–73, 76–77
5. PR Watch [accessed 19 September 2003] Introduction. http://www.prwatch.org
6. Grabbe, J O [accessed 19 September 2003] How to create a war. http://www.aci.net/kalliste/hkwar.htm
7. Baumhart, R (1968) *An Honest Profit: What businessmen say about ethics in business*, Holt, Rinehart & Winston
8. Global Alliance for Public Relations and Communication Management [accessed 19 September 2003] Global Procotol. http://www.globalpr.org/knowledge/ethics/protocol.asp
9. Maister, D (2000) *True Professionalism: The courage to care about your people, your clients, and your career*, Touchstone Press, New York, pp 16, 17

2

Untangling the web: the 'truth' and other strangers

A lie gets halfway around the world before the truth has a chance to get its pants on.

Sir Winston Churchill

In the autumn of 2000 the Canadian Broadcasting Corporation (CBC) aired promos for a new television show. 'When their lips move you know they're lying', said the voice-over. Whom, exactly, was he talking about? The 'they' to whom the voice referred were the protagonists on an absurd sitcom titled *PR* which debuted that autumn, much to the chagrin of every public relations practitioner who had the misfortune of seeing an episode or two. Then to add to the embarrassment the companion web site told the world: 'If they told the truth, they'd be out of business.'

While many PR practitioners may have had have had as much trouble believing in the star's wardrobe as her outrageously inaccurate depiction of what public relations is all about, like it or not the notion of failing to tell the truth, or even spinning the facts, is part of the public's image of public relations. And who can blame them when this is the media image that is cultivated?

This raises two questions. First, is the public really so wrong? And second, what part *does* truth telling play in the ethical foundations of public relations? We'll deal with question two first.

AN EPIDEMIC OF LYING

Everyone lies. This has become a fact of the modern human condition. And you need not protest your own absolute honesty. If you have ever told a friend (or spouse or sibling) that you like that gruesome sweater or that obnoxious girlfriend, or even said something non-committal, you've chosen a path that is just short of absolute honesty. You have your reasons for behaving this way, you say, and you might even find an ethicist or two who can accept your motivation for such dishonesty. Clearly, we all draw the line both personally and professionally. There are some lies we will tell, whereas there are others that seem just beyond the pale. What is unclear is the difference between that little lie that seems so unimportant at the time and the important ones that have significant consequences. The truth, the whole truth and nothing but the truth seems relegated to the courtroom oath.

Most recognized religions, where many of us receive our first introduction to values, expound on the requirement to tell the truth. The Ten Commandments taught many PR professionals their first lesson in truth telling. Most other religious traditions, however, also have guidelines regarding the virtue of telling the truth. For example, there is the Buddhist Eightfold Path, one point of which is 'right speech', the first element of which is abstaining from false speech. Indeed, you'd be hard-pressed to find a religious tradition that did not touch on this as a fundamental moral principle. Yet we continue to tell those 'little white lies' in our personal lives, with an almost inevitable spill-over into our professional lives.

THE 'TRUTH' IN PUBLIC RELATIONS

Public relations is a public communication function and as such its practitioners have responsibilities that speak to the greater good – whether we like it or not. The public are sceptical of the truth of what is communicated to them and we really don't have a right to clog up the channels of public communication with more untruths or half-truths. Codes of ethics of professional associations of public relations practitioners provide chapter and verse on the need for the truth.

For example, the Chartered Institute of Public Relations (CIPR) Code of Conduct says: 'Members of the Institute of Public Relations agree to... deal honestly and fairly in business with employers, employees, clients, fellow professionals, other professions and the public.'[1] The Canadian Public Relations Society's Code of Professional Standards is even more specific. It states: 'A member shall practice the highest standards of honesty, accuracy, integrity and truth, and shall not knowingly disseminate false or misleading information', and goes on to drill this down even further: 'Members shall not make extravagant claims or unfair comparisons, nor assume credit for ideas and words not their own.'[2]

So it seems that telling the truth, although often deemed to be a casualty in the search for new and better ways to disseminate messages and persuade publics, is an important aspect of ethical public relations. Defining what the truth *is* in public relations, just as in other aspects of our lives, however, is a challenge.

In his discussion of truth and the act of communication, University of Oregon professor Thomas Bivins suggests that 'to lie to someone is to lead them to act in a manner in which they would not have acted had you told them the truth.'[3] Given that one of the objectives of our business is often to persuade publics to change their behaviour, we need to be very careful of achieving what could be considered an ethical outcome through unethical means. Defining the truth is clearly the challenge.

A public relations researcher at Florida International University tried to do just that.[4] He wanted to determine where to draw that line through a very murky area by surveying public relations educators' opinions about what constitutes 'truthful communication' in public relations practice. First, the PR educators who participated in the survey clearly defined it to be lying when PR practitioners 'make factual declarations that they know to be untrue'. This would seem fairly self-evident: if you are fully aware that what you're saying is not truthful, then this is a clear example of a lie. Being misleading or even evasive is a different story, however. The truth or lack thereof in these situations is less clear. It seems that the motivation behind withholding information is the key to truth telling in public relations – not unlike that little white lie about your friend's awful sweater that we discussed earlier.

There is one situation in which it seems that telling the whole truth is not the most ethical course of action. If telling the truth outright is likely to harm one or more publics, then it is reasonable to conclude that it is probably more ethical to avoid full disclosure. After all, one of the first principles of ethics in any situation is to do no harm – a principle that we'll discuss in greater depth later. Often, however, the distinction about whether truth or harm trumps the other requires a judgement call; it is the application of such judgement that calls upon the ethical maturity and development of the decision-maker.

All of this seems like so much logical common sense when it comes to ethics. Consider my own surprise to find a piece written by a Canadian public relations practitioner that was posted for at least two years on the CPRS website suggesting that taking on the role of advocate, which is at the heart of modern public relations, is somehow in conflict with truth telling, which furthermore isn't important anyway, as long as we're doing what the client wants.

Public relations consultant Peter O'Malley seems to believe that the Canadian Public Relations Society's Code of Professional Standards' reference to honesty and integrity may be inspiring, but 'ignores what public relations is all about'.[5]

O'Malley justifies this claim with an analogy between lawyers and PR practitioners. This spurious comparison often surfaces when PR practitioners wish to justify questionable behaviour. It is a widely held principle in civilized cultures that everyone has the right to legal representation. Perhaps it is even an important principle that everyone has a right to have professional public relations counsel to make his or her voice heard in the arena of public communication, thus facilitating access. But the analogy breaks down when it comes to the lawyer representing clients whom he or she knows to be guilty. What the lawyer is then supporting is not a loyalty to and belief in the client; rather that lawyer is upholding a belief in a legal system and everyone's right to due process. No such infrastructure exists for public relations. Thus, we have logically to assume that public relations practitioners are not bound to do whatever their clients bid them to do, and in fact are behaving unethically if they lie on their clients' behalf, even if it is at their behest. O'Malley's contention is that if you want to be an ethical public relations practitioner, you 'choose to serve clients whose self-defined interests are, in [your] view correct. And [you] don't serve those whose purposes and interests are incorrect. Period.'[6]

It is difficult to argue with him on this point. However, all this simplistic view of ethics does is reinforce the public image of PR as a less than ethical industry; it fails to move us forward into a future where public relations' role truly is to develop mutually beneficial relationships between organizations and their publics whose foundation is trust – the only true foundation for mutual benefit.

American philosophy professor Mitchell Green of the University of Virginia takes a broader view of the ethics of truth telling when he says 'truth telling is not a matter of speaking the truth but it is rather a matter of speaking what one believes to be the truth' and further 'one can mislead without lying.'[7] The issue of misleading is an especially important one in public relations. If failing to disclose information, regardless of the motivation, leads the public to a wrong conclusion and this was a predictable situation (or worse, was the objective), then it is as ethically questionable as telling an outright lie.

CAN YOU PREDICT HONESTY?

If we truly believe that the ability and motivation to tell the truth are honourable if not essential characteristics for success in the field of public relations, wouldn't it be useful if we could tell who is most likely to be honest? Consider how useful it might be if we could screen potential students in PR or even applicants for jobs? Perhaps surprisingly, there is at least one predictor.

Take a look around your office. Who among your own colleagues (and don't leave yourself out of this evaluation) do you think is most likely to cheat? Who would be the one who might take credit for others' work? Which of your writers would be most likely to fail to cite the sources of material combed from the work of others? Which one in your office might be persuaded to make up quotes and statistics?

If you think there is no way to tell the ones most likely to dwell on the moral high ground from those bottom-feeders who don't seem to have any conscience, you are probably unaware of the recent studies that have tried to do just that: figure out the predictors for people who are more likely than others to be the cheats of the business world. It could help the next time you try to fill that vacant position in your department.

First, we'll define a cheat the way most dictionaries do: someone who acts dishonestly, who deceives others or attempts to defraud. Now we'll take a trip back to where cheating first seems to become an issue.

It seems that today's university and college students are just as concerned as you are about the amount of cheating that seems to be running rampant in the modern business world. The evidence: a study reported in *Business Week* magazine found that a whopping 84 per cent of a group of 1,100 students surveyed believe that the United States is having a business crisis.[8] However, when the same students were asked about their own ethics, they sang a different tune.

Over half the students admitted to cheating (cheating on exams, plagiarism, etc) and fewer than 20 per cent of them said that they would report a classmate whom they knew had cheated. It is interesting to note that these students were members of the organization *Students in Free Enterprise*, an organization active on some 1,300 college and university campuses in 33 countries that purports to teach principles of (among other things) business ethics.[9]

Perhaps you might now be considering that just because someone cheats in college or university does not necessarily mean that he or she is likely to be unethical in business. Indeed, when asked, many students – even my own – just don't consider college or university to be the real world and the competitive pressures are legion, all of which in their view seems to justify cheating while a student. The story, however, does not end there.

All of this new information about the students of today, who are in many ways idealistic as students often are, is very interesting in light of a slightly older study reported in 1993 that tried to determine whether there might be a relationship between academic dishonesty (cheating) and later dishonesty in business dealings.[10] The researchers found that, indeed, those MBA students who admitted to having engaged in a wide range of academic dishonesty also admitted to a wide range of work-related dishonesty. Given the recent consternation about the almost epidemic proportions of academic cheating going on today on campuses around the world, and the apparent widespread belief that there's really nothing wrong with it (perhaps unless you get caught), I believe that there is reason to be very concerned about the future of ethical conduct in our business world. So, maybe that notation on a new graduate's academic transcript that indicates an academic offence might actually be important to the potential employer. But these are only the ones who get caught. There are other predictors, though.

Lisa Yoon, writing in the online publication *CFO.com*, reported on the world of golf for business executives.[11] She reported on the results of a study of 401 executives carried out for Starwood that found that 97 per cent of those surveyed considered golf to be a good way to establish a close relationship with a business colleague – but with sizable ulterior motives at play alongside the drivers and the putters.

'Twenty per cent of executives surveyed said they would let a client beat them,' Yoon writes, 'if they thought it would get them more business; 87 per cent gamble while golfing; and a whopping 82 per cent of executives admit to cheating on the golf course.' The clincher, however, was that 86 per cent of these executives also admitted to cheating in business.

Dishonesty seems to be a way of life for some people in the business world of today – a kind of Machiavellian style of achieving power and success perhaps. However, in the field of public relations, where honesty has not always been the hallmark of the practice, perhaps we need to be even more vigilant than others that our communication is not only honest, but perceived to be honest as well.

If you are faced with the prospect of publicizing something that you know to be untrue, there is little doubt that in the court of public opinion there is no justification for this kind of unethical behaviour. On the other hand, there may be ethical justification for partial disclosure so long as it does not mislead the public or harm anyone. When you finish reading this chapter you might consider assessing your own view of honesty by answering for yourself the series of questions posed in Figure 2.1. Of course, self-assessment requires that you at least be honest with yourself.

Your honesty assessment

Consider the following activities. If you are currently not a student, think back about the years when you were. If you are currently a student, you shouldn't have any trouble remembering if these are activities in which you engage.

If you have done any of the following **even once**, place a check mark in the box:

- ☐ taken crib notes into an exam (that wasn't open-book) even if you didn't use them;
- ☐ used your crib notes during an exam;
- ☐ used material from a source without acknowledging it (quotes or not);
- ☐ lied to an instructor about your reason for missing a deadline;
- ☐ bought a paper (either from the Internet or not) and submitted it largely unchanged;
- ☐ used material gleaned from (inadvertently) glancing at someone else's exam.

If you are currently working and not a student, continue with the following, placing a check mark in the box beside any activity in which you have ever engaged **even once**. If you are a student, you might consider which of them you are likely to do based on your behaviour as a student:

- ☐ taken credit for an accomplishment that was not truly yours;
- ☐ made a statement in written material (such as a news release or client pitch) that was not strictly honest;
- ☐ taken office supplies home and used them for other than work-related activities;
- ☐ lied to a supervisor about your reason for missing a deadline;
- ☐ used information gleaned from (inadvertently) glancing at a colleague's computer screen;
- ☐ failed to acknowledge the source of information.

Now that you have two groups of check marks, compare the two lists.

Figure 2.1   *Your honesty assessment*

ONE PRINCIPLE AMONG SEVERAL

If telling the truth is a cornerstone of public relations as a communication industry, is it enough of a yardstick to judge the ethics of our behaviour? As an ethical principle, it is a start and constitutes one of those fundamental assumptions about behaving ethically, but it is only one of several such principles that are necessary for the evaluation of the ethics of our actions. Truth telling, then is one of the five *Pillars of Public Relations Ethics*.

THE PILLARS OF PUBLIC
RELATIONS ETHICS

Veracity (to tell the truth)

Non-maleficence (to do no harm)

Beneficence (to do good)

Confidentiality (to respect privacy)

Fairness (to be fair and socially responsible)

Think of these principles as the pillars that carry the weight of ethical decision-making in public relations practice.

These pillars or principles evolved from an analysis of the ways in which long-held ethical principles of bioethics might be applied to the field of public relations practice. The so-called 'four principles' in bioethics are non-maleficence, beneficence, autonomy and justice.[12,13] When business scholars examined these principles and analysed the extent to which they might be more widely useful, they concluded that as an ethics tool, they provide an important analytical tool, helping to 'frame controversies'[14] in the world of business not just in medicine.[15] Indeed, they can be applied to all manner of corporate communication strategies and as such could more broadly be termed the *Five Pillars of Ethics in Public Communication*.[16]

The concept of *doing no harm* as a fundamental principle of moral behaviour has already surfaced in our discussion. As a pillar of ethics in the field of public relations, it provides us with a one-question analysis of any decision we choose to make before we make it. *Will my actions harm others?* Obviously, this isn't the final analysis, but it is the place to start. We ought to avoid doing harm to others as far as is possible; certainly no intentional harm should be done and we should avoid foreseeable harm. Sometimes, the harm that we cause is both unintended and unforeseen. In that case, our actions cannot be deemed to be unethical – just unfortunate and perhaps regrettable.

The concept of *doing good* is a corollary of avoiding harm but it is a more proactive tenet and speaks of a kind of altruistic ethical intent. Looking for opportunities to do good can be helpful in making decisions about the relative morality of public relations activities. For example, if faced with two or more relatively 'good' alternatives to reach a conclusion in a situation, you might consider which of them is likely to do the most good. In addition, applying this principle to everyday public relations practice, we might reasonably conclude that ethical PR seeks out opportunities to do good. For example, when developing a community relations programme, seeking to sponsor the charitable event that could actually do the most good for the public rather than the one that does little material good but improves your image would be construed to be the most ethical approach. Finding a balance between the two is the challenge for the creative PR practitioner (see Chapter 14 for a further examination of this principle in action).

The next pillar, *respecting the privacy of others* and keeping confidential information that is of a confidential nature is clearly germane to ethical decision-making in any public communication function. Unfortunately, this is rarely a simple matter of considering an individual's right to privacy when dealing with journalists who believe in the public's right to know and further believe that this takes precedence over what you might define as an individual's – or even an organization's – right to privacy. 'In public communication, there is often a conflict between the need to tell the truth and the equally important principle to keep private those matters that are not of a public nature.'[15] Ethical decision-making is nothing if not a balancing act, as we shall see.

The final pillar upon which public relations ethics is based in my view is the concept of *fairness and social responsibility*. Trying to respect all individuals and society in our decisions is an attempt to be fair. At times, it seems that our role as organizational advocates flies in the face of the requirement to be fair, but as we'll see in Chapter 13, that does not have to be the case.

These fundamental principles provide us with a bridge between the theoretical underpinnings of ethics as a philosophical field of study and the way these theories might be operationalized into a practical tool for everyday practice. They provide a first pass at analysing a situation to determine its ethical implications before we move on to the more difficult part of ethics in action: namely actually making decisions that we can live with and defend to others. We'll get to that process in more detail in Chapter 15. But before we do that, we need to continue to develop an underlying framework and take a hard look at ethics in professional practice.

Perhaps it would be useful to consider Mark Twain's simple philosophy about truth telling: 'If you tell the truth, you don't have to remember anything.'

Notes

1. Chartered Institute of Public Relations Code of Conduct [accessed 25 October 2007] http://www.cipr.co.uk/Membership/conduct/index.htm

2. Canadian Public Relations Society Code of Professional Standards [accessed 25 October 2007] http://www.cprs.ca/AboutCPRS/e_code.htm

3. Bivins, T (2004) *Mixed Media: Moral distinctions in advertising, public relations and journalism*, Lawrence Erlbaum, Mahwah, NJ, p 121

4. Martinson, David L [accessed 19 May 1998] Educators define telling the 'truth' in PR, published by the Association for Education in Journalism and Mass Communication No 33, November 1993, http://www.usc.edu/schools/annenburg/asc/projects/prd/33martin.html

5. O'Malley, Peter [accessed 25 October 2007] In praise of secrecy, http://www.cprs.ca/cprspraise.html

6. O'Malley, In praise of secrecy

7. Green, Mitchell [accessed 5 August 2003] Truthtelling, http://www.people.virginia.edu/~msg6m/TRUTHTEL.pdf

8. Weisul, K and Merritt, J (12 December 2002) You mean cheating is wrong? *Business Week*, p 8

9. See Students in Free Enterprise website, http://www.sife.org

10. Sims, R (1993) The relationship between academic dishonesty and unethical business practices, *Journal of Education for Business*, **68** (4), pp 207–211

11. Yoon, Lisa [accessed 25 October 2007] Double-dealing duffers (October 2002), http://www.cfo.com/article.cfm/3006790?f'search

12. Jonsen, A (1994) *Clinical Ethics and the Four Principles*, Wiley, New York

13. Preston, R (1994) *The Four Principles and their Use*, Wiley, New York

14. Fisher, J (2001) Lessons for business ethics from bioethics, *Journal of Bioethics* **34** (1), pp 15–24

15. Parsons, P (2007) Integrating ethics with strategy: analyzing disease branding, *Corporate Communications: An International Journal*, **12** (3), pp 267–279

16. Parsons, p. 274

3

Truth, trust and the virtue of being 'good'

Trust is the lubrication that makes it possible for organizations to work.

Warren Bennis

Telling the 'truth' isn't always enough. It may be a good place to start in a field like public relations but it falls short of fulfilling your ethical responsibilities as a professional in a public communication function. Sometimes you tell the truth and you are still left with a dilemma. Trust is the key element in the development of your employer's or client's relationships with their publics, but it is equally an important part of your own professional relationships. With trust, much can be accomplished; without trust, your efforts to accomplish anything will feel like an uphill battle.

TRUTH AND TRUST

To understand the relationship between telling the truth and the subsequent ability to nurture a trusting relationship, we need to examine exactly what trust consists of. *Webster's Dictionary* defines trust as 'a confident reliance on the integrity, veracity, or justice of another; confidence; faith'.[1] The definition itself clearly defines the relationship between truth and trust. If you don't tell the truth, then your publics, once they are aware of this, have difficulty trusting you. If a public does not trust you, then the relationship deteriorates. It's as simple as that.

What is less simple, however, is determining what truth really means in business today.

German philosopher Immanuel Kant, whose work is widely taught in ethics courses, believed that ethics consists of fulfilling our duties categorically. For example, as far as Kant was concerned, telling the truth was one of those categorical duties. We have an obligation to tell the truth – *under all circumstances*. In today's world of business, it seems clear that telling the truth is sometimes overshadowed by other duties. We have already established the fact that telling the truth, the whole truth and nothing but the truth is for the courtroom and that sometimes we have a duty to withhold information to protect people, a decision that clearly requires a judgement call, but when does even telling the truth mislead and contribute to mistrust between organizations and their publics? Here's a case that illustrates this point.

THE LIMITS OF ORGANIZATIONAL RESPONSIBILITY

The story was not an uncommon one:

> On November 1, 1978, newspapers throughout America were saturated with a remarkable medical news story – the discovery of what was reported to be a new non-steroidal anti-inflammatory drug to treat arthritis, a painful chronic ailment that plagues more than 25 million Americans.[2]

This public relations story began with a news release that was issued by the PR office of the drug firm in question, inventors of the 'new' drug. The news release read in part: 'Relief of the pain and disabling joint symptoms of five major arthritic diseases is now possible with a single anti-inflammatory drug that has been found to be even better tolerated than aspirin.'[3] Later in the release, the senior vice-president for science technology referred to the drug as 'a major advance' that would bring benefit to a 'much broader range of patients'.

News stories that subsequently covered this 'major advance' were unwelcome by a medical community that saw the coverage as highly exaggerated and found themselves, with no prior notice about this drug, explaining to desperate patients that this was not the magic bullet that they had been awaiting. It even sparked correspondence in the *New England Journal of Medicine,* where one physician wrote, 'we believe the company has a responsibility not to allow this type of deception'.[4]

Was he right? Was this a deception? What are the limits of an organization's responsibility? And what are the implications for the ongoing trust in the relationship between the company and one of its most important publics (in this case physicians)?

The most important cold fact in the situation is that the news release was factually accurate. There was no lie; the information was the truth. But this still does not answer the question of whether or not a deception took place. Whereas it is common practice in the pharmaceutical industry to herald the release of a new drug with considerable fanfare, including media releases and conferences, it has been less usual – especially at the time of this story – for them to announce the release of new formulations of drugs that aren't substantially different from competitors' products. Arthritis sufferers, a vulnerable public if ever there was one, interpreted the fanfare in a predictable manner – they flocked to their doctors in search of this magic bullet only to be greeted by doctors who failed to see it that way.

Media critic Morris Wolfe has been quoted frequently for his observation 'It's easier and less costly to change the way people think about reality than it is to change reality.' Joel Bleifuss, writing about the public relations industry in the *Utne Reader,* suggests 'Manipulating the public's perception of reality takes special skills.'[5] Of course, he contends that the people who possess those special manipulative skills are PR practitioners.

This is one of those situations where telling the truth isn't enough and the application of the term manipulative may be warranted. It would be easy for the organization to blame the media for their interpretation of the news release. In fact, this is always the easy way out. But the easy way out is rarely an example of doing the right thing even when no one is looking.

Clearly, there are times in every PR practitioner's career when the media do, in fact, get it wrong. Unfortunately, even when the message isn't within your control, the result is a public whose trust in you and your organization begins to deteriorate. To begin to see how you can deal with this particular ethical underpinning, it's important to consider the parties to whom you, as a public relations practitioner, owe duties.

TO WHOM ARE YOU LOYAL?

We might define a loyalty as 'a constituent to whom the public relations practitioner owes a duty and who, in return, places a trust in the practitioner'.[6] Again the issue of trust rears its head. Whereas it is true that when dealing in specific public relations situations you might consider each individual public to be a 'loyalty' that you have a duty towards, in general there are four overriding loyalties in the everyday practice of public relations.

One of the first duties that may come to mind is duty to your employer or client. You took on a particular position with a contract, either written or implied. You do a particular job and your employer or client provides you with monetary compensation. It's a simple relationship when put in these terms. However, to what extent is it necessary for you to be loyal under these circumstances? If the employer says do something, do you do it? Blindly? Without consideration of consequences to others or yourself? What happens when your employer or client expects you to do something that you know will erode the trust of others?

If you consider the case of the newly released drug that we discussed at the beginning of the chapter, you might consider specifically that your loyalty (your duty) to your employer who pays your salary just might conflict with your duties to others such as doctors and patients who trust your organization and its products. It then becomes a matter of placing your loyalties in order of priority – and this is not a fixed ranking. Situations can alter the priorities.

Arguably even more important ethically than your duty to your employer or client is your duty to society. This is the key to social responsibility. In the drug release situation, consideration should be given to the impact that this kind of communication tactic has on the social fabric and the extent to which society can trust an organization that is perceived to mislead.

Another loyalty that you might consider is your duty to your profession. Public relations as a professional discipline has a public image that is less than spotless in the area of ethics. As we move forward in dispelling some of the long-held opinions about our field, we have a duty to ensure that we practise our profession in an ethical manner. Consideration of public relations as your professional field needs always to be in the back of your mind when you are trying to make well-founded moral decisions.

Finally, and perhaps where you might have begun this examination of loyalties, is your duty to yourself. Indeed, some people believe that one of the most common, if not the most common ethical dilemma that will face all PR practitioners at some point in their career is to have to make a choice between what the employer or client is asking of them and what they as individuals, and based on their own personal value systems, know to be right.

Clearly, then, as a public relations practitioner, you have duties to yourself, your employer or client, your profession and to society as a whole. Juggling these duties can be a full-time job when trying to practise PR in an ethical manner (Figure 3.1).

Juggling your loyalties

Figure 3.1 *Juggling your loyalties*

In another example, consider the public relations instructor who provides career counselling to his graduating students. He knows from years of experience in the industry that those students who complete the two-year programme right after high school, rather than after a university degree or several years of work experience, are not viewed by potential employers as mature enough and will therefore generally have more difficulty finding employment in the PR field than their older, more experienced classmates. So, he counsels them to consider pursuing a university degree and putting off their job search. His boss tells him he can't do this as it contravenes the school's obligation to treat everyone equally.

The instructor's duty to his students, clearly a priority public, is at least as important as his duty to his employer – hence, the ethical dilemma.

If you consider the 'pillars of ethical public relations' that we discussed in Chapter 2, you might notice that there is a potential here to transgress one of them: to do no harm. A strong argument could be made in both the drug company's situation and the instructor's that there is a potential for harm. The patients could be harmed by the possibility of false hope, and the students could be harmed if they are not provided with honest, candid information based on sound experience of the instructor – the ethical approach. Ethical living is a balancing act. And juggling the components until we find the right balance is a delicate business.

Clearly, our publics need to be able to trust us. Being certain that our organizations will do them no harm is crucial to that trust. But finding that balance requires a close understanding of how you as an individual approach thinking about ethics.

THE VIRTUE OF BEING 'GOOD'

Authors who write about ethics often categorize people according to their particular, individual orientations towards making decisions. Some of us are oriented towards thinking about the potential outcomes (more about that 'utilitarian' approach in Chapter 6), while others are more likely to be guided by the processes and rules they believe are most appropriate for making those decisions (more about this 'deontology' in Chapter 5). The third way that guides some people's approaches to ethical behaviour is focused on neither processes nor outcomes; rather their approach takes its guidance from those personal characteristics that are held in the highest esteem when it comes to 'doing the right thing'. In other words, they might use the following question to determine the ethical approach to a situation:

If I were a 'good' person, what would I do?

which raises the next question...

What characteristics does a 'good' person possess? If I know what these characteristics are and I cultivate them in myself, I will be able to make moral decisions, regardless of rules or outcomes.

It may sound easy enough, but in practice it's a lot harder to figure out.

This approach is called *Virtue Ethics* and one of its earliest proponents was Aristotle. The problem with being virtuous and depending on that for ethical guidance is determining what those ethical virtues are. Aristotle suggested that if you consider the potential extremes of behavioural responses, then finding the middle ground identifies the virtuous stance. Professor Thomas Bivins provides the following examples: '... the middle ground between cowardice and foolhardiness would be courage. The mean between shamelessness and bashfulness is modesty; and between stinginess and wastefulness lies generosity'.[7] So, if we were able to identify a series of virtues that would make us 'good' persons, and then sought to behave in a manner congruent with those virtues, the outcome would be virtuous – or ethical – behaviour, at least from the virtue ethics point of view.

Manuel Velasquez, Claire Andre and Thomas Shanks from Santa Clara University in California suggest the following as a way of understanding this approach:

'Virtues' are attitudes, dispositions, or character traits that enable us to be and to act in ways that develop this potential. They enable us to pursue the ideals we have adopted. Honesty, courage, compassion, generosity, fidelity, integrity, fairness, self-control, and prudence are all examples of virtues.[8]

Consideration of what each of us as an individual might believe to be the important characteristics – or virtues – of a 'good' person and which of these we either possess or wish to cultivate is a good exercise. For example, you might ask yourself: what kind of person would I most like to interact with? Taking this a step further, you might consider the extent to which these characteristics might affect your actual ethical behaviour in specific situations. Anything that we do to know our moral selves better is a step towards ensuring an ethical stance in both our personal and professional undertakings.

In the end, isn't a moral organization, which can only be so if it is a collection of moral individuals, the kind of organization that publics can trust?

Notes

1. *Webster's Dictionary* (1992) PMC Publishing Company, New York, p 1038
2. Heussner, R and Salmon, M (1988) *Warning: The media may be harmful to your health*, Andrews & McMeel, Kansas City, p 62
3. Quoted in Heussner and Salmon, p 62
4. Wasner, C and Kotzin, B (1979) 'Sulindac public relations deplored', *New England Journal of Medicine*, **300**, p 373
5. Bleifuss, J (1994) Flack attack, *Utne Reader*, January–February, p 72
6. Parsons, P (1993) Framework for analysis of conflicting loyalties, *Public Relations Review*, **19** (1), p 50
7. Bivins, T (2004) *Mixed Media: Moral distinctions in advertising, public relations and journalism*, Lawrence Erlbaum, Mahwah, NJ, p 99
8. Velasquez, M, Andre, C and Shanks, T [accessed 30 October 2007] *Ethics and Virtue*, Markkula Centre for Applied Ethics, Santa Clara University, http://www.scu.edu/ethics/practicing/decision/ethics andvirtue.html

4

Whose rights are right?

Safeguarding the rights of others is the most noble and beautiful end of a human being.

Kahlil Gibran

The beaches were beautiful, the palm trees glorious – and after a prolonged and nasty Canadian winter, a week in the Bahamas was just what I needed. After only a week home, my tan began to fade, but thoughts of idyllic hours by the pool reading an absorbing novel (instead of ethics and public relations literature) were still clear. And so were the olfactory memories, from inside every Bahamian restaurant, on every patio, at every pool side, in every lobby and even in the washrooms. Cigarette and even cigar smoke filled our nostrils at every turn.

As a die-hard Canadian who lives in one of the many cities in this country where smoking in public is all but a distant memory, I hold close to my heart the right not to be forced to breathe in second-hand smoke at every turn. Recent trips to the United States and abroad, however, had brought home to me that this seems not to be a widely acknowledged personal right. So, perhaps a right is not necessarily a right at all. Or is it? Do you even recognize when you face conflicts of rights situations in your day-to-day public relations practice? This brief chapter provides but a beginning introduction to the concept of rights so that you can be aware of what others may claim when you are faced with making ethical decisions.

RIGHTS AND RESPONSIBILITIES

There are human rights, patients' rights, employee rights, students' rights, women's rights, reproductive rights – the list goes on, although, to be fair, some people believe that there are rights that every human being has, and the concept of special rights for any specific group is unethical in itself. That said, what exactly is a right and how do I get one?

The term 'right' has become so ubiquitous that it appears to be losing some of its power and meaning. It seems that a right is fundamental to our understanding of what individuals can expect in terms of ethical behaviour towards them in a particular society. Clearly, even from my own simple example, although I may consider it my right to breathe non-cigarette-smoke-polluted air when I'm dining or at any other time for that matter, is it really a right? Or should I just stay at home and eat there, or perhaps wear a mask when in the company of smokers?

One way of looking at it is that a right is the freedom to act or be treated in a particular way, where this right is protected and endorsed by a higher authority – in the case of human rights, for example, a constitution or declaration of human rights and freedoms. All other rights claimed must be justified by these fundamental declarations. And to add to that, these higher authorities that grant rights then have the responsibility to uphold those rights.

Within businesses or industries, declarations of rights might be granted to cover specialized issues. For example, in the healthcare industry, patients' bills of rights are rampant. The healthcare industry itself, prompted in many cases by consumer groups, has developed these rights and therefore the healthcare industry and the groups who determine these rights constitute the higher authority to which the patient should appeal if that person is unable to exercise a particular right.

In business, your organization might have a declaration of your employees' rights – the right to a safe working environment, the right to work without harassment, for example. The organization itself grants these rights and as a result has the responsibility to uphold them. But these declarations don't mean that your organization has the responsibility to ensure a safe working environment in a competitor across the street. It does mean that these rights apply equally to *all* your employees.

The bottom line is that you do not have a right unless I or someone else grants it to you. You may claim rights until you're blue in the face, but until someone agrees with you, the right doesn't exist. You cannot claim a right – it has to be given to you.

Ever since I was an undergraduate student, I've thought of a right as a justified claim. In other words, it isn't enough simply to declare that you have a specific right (although given the number of people who do so it might seem that easy). You must have substantial justification for that right and others who would then have a duty to uphold your right must agree. Generally, that justification comes in the form of one of those higher authorities that recognizes a duty to uphold your right. But what about those rights claimed as protected and endorsed by higher authorities that are perhaps more nebulous, such as religious belief, custom, God or even conscience? Who, then, can justify them and uphold these rights? Whereas members of a particular society might be able to agree on certain rights assured in law, there are other rights that lead to considerable disagreement.

Eighteenth-century philosopher Immanuel Kant, whose categorical imperative we discussed in Chapter 3, had very specific ideas about the moral value of human beings and his perspective often informs today's discussions about rights. He said that people must always be treated as ends, rather than as a means to an end. If people are treated as a means to an end, then their personal dignity isn't being respected. This kind of argument is what provides support for the disagreements about supposed rights that are granted by those more ambiguous higher authorities.

WHEN MY RIGHT CONFLICTS WITH YOURS

One of the most frequently cited categories of ethical dilemmas that face us today are those situations where the rights one person claims seem to conflict directly with those rights claimed by another person.

Thus, if I have, under law, the right to the pursuit of health, then clearly I have the right to be protected from someone else's cigarette smoke. There is ample medical and scientific evidence to support the belief that second-hand smoke does, indeed, contribute to overall ill health. But if the smoker has the right to the pursuit of happiness (as US citizens claim under their constitution, for example), and smoking a cigarette makes this person happy, then don't we have a conflict of rights? Is someone's health more important than someone else's happiness? Clearly, in this situation, since it is my health we're talking about, I'm likely to believe that to be so. If I were the smoker claiming that cigarettes were my route to achieving happiness, I'd probably disagree, and thus we have the classic conflict of rights dilemma.

CONFLICTING RIGHTS IN PUBLIC RELATIONS

One of the classic rights conflict situations in public relations is when the right to privacy of individuals within organizations conflicts with the public's right to know, as frequently articulated by the media. Let's look at some situations:

- One of your managers has been rumoured to be dating a movie star. She wishes to keep her personal life private and your organization's policy has been to uphold an employee's right to personal privacy. The media have got wind of this juicy story and want details, believing in their right to access when dealing with a public figure such as a movie star.
- The same manager again, but now she's been accused of sexual harassment against one of her subordinates. A woman in your town has never been accused of this before. A reporter received an inside tip and wants details. He thinks the public has a right to know.
- The same manager again, but she is now accused of embezzlement. Media are again on the trail of a story.

Whose rights prevail in these situations? The public's? The media's? The employee's? Or does your organization have rights? (Most ethics authors believe that only people have rights, but you might be able to argue that an organization is nothing if not a collection of people.)

There is a whole area of ethics that is focused on a rights-based approach to ethical decision-making. We have merely scratched the surface of this topic, but it's a start and adds one more concept to your evolving framework which will eventually form the basis for your own ethical decision-making.

5

The trouble with rules

Integrity has no need of rules.

Albert Camus

I don't know anyone who has not, from time to time, called upon that old cliché: 'Rules were made to be broken.' The trouble is, however, that when it comes to ethical behaviour, there is often monumental bewilderment about what those rules are to begin with, how to apply them in everyday life and if it is ever appropriate to break them. In this chapter we'll examine what kinds of rules might be brought to bear in making ethical decisions and the difference between being a rule-dominated ethical decision-maker versus one who is more likely to judge situations based on their individual merits.

RULES RULE OUR LIVES

Rules are a part of our so-called civilized existence from the cradle to the grave. We face family rules, school rules and eventually those rules to which all of us must subscribe or face serious consequences – society's laws. (Although by definition rules and laws are not exactly the same thing, based on common usage of the terms, for the purposes of our discussion, we'll consider laws to be a kind of rule.) And while it seems that if we had moral laws and consequences it might be easier to police ethical behaviour, it would actually be much more difficult to act in an ethical manner in modern society.

Take the case of the school bus driver with a bus full of children. One beautiful autumn day, the bus driver ferries his load of exuberant children along a road towards a set of traffic lights. As the bus moves down the hill towards the intersection, the bus driver glances in his rear view mirror and notices with horror that there is a tractor trailer bearing down on him, seemingly without any intention or perhaps ability to stop. Another glance forward tells the bus driver that the light has just turned red. Normally, he follows the laws of the land to the letter. A red light means stop. Our society tells us that we must obey the laws. What should he do?

OK. This is an easy one. He considers his responsibility to the children, checks for oncoming traffic and barrels through the red light, breaking the law. He did something illegal, but you'd be hard-pressed to find anyone who truly believes that in this case the law should not take into account this specific situation. There were mitigating circumstances.

Rules and laws are like that. It would be a huge advantage to us if we always knew how to do the right thing, or perhaps more to the point, if we always knew what we *ought to do*, particularly since this is the fundamental objective of ethical decision-making. But not all situations are the same. In fact, in ethics, there are two distinct and often opposing approaches to ethical decision-making. One is based on the belief that what one *ought to do* is adopt and follow a set of ethical rules. The second approach suggests that what one *ought to do* is apply ethical rules and principles based on the specific circumstances of the situation.

Which approach ought one to adopt?

THOSE DARN DEONTOLOGISTS

The first approach is what many people refer to as *rule-based ethics*. This approach to making decisions suggests that being ethical is a matter of accepting that as individual human beings we have a *duty* to do certain things. These 'certain things' are based on ethical principles and form the rules that you should follow. Further, as an ethical thinker with this perspective, you would apply these rules equally and fairly to all. For example, if one of the rules is that you have a duty to be honest, then you must be honest in all situations.

The rules that people adopt as their moral standards are often set out for them by others such as organized religions (think: the Ten

Commandments). For members of a particular professional group, they might think of their rules as those set out by professional associations such as the Chartered Institute of Public Relations (think: the Code of Ethics). These codes of conduct, however, tend to be broad guidelines that are themselves based on more specific rules. They are developed based on selected universal ethical principles and the values of those creating them; they are codified and presented as the rules of engagement. We'll discuss codes of ethics more thoroughly in Chapter 8.

A rule-based approach to ethics, with its consistent application of dogmatic ethical principles or rules, does have a certain appeal. If you do not feel fully qualified to be making moral judgements or comfortable changing the application of the rules to fit a situation, this approach is reassuring. In fact, this approach may appear at first glance to provide a just, equitable way to ensure equivalent decisions in similar situations. Indeed, your duties clearly define what you ought to do. But consider the plight of our bus driver. If a law is a law is a law – well, you can see what can happen.

THE REAL TROUBLE WITH RULES

On the surface, in our day-to-day practice, it may seem useful and comforting to have a cookbook-style guide to help us solve ethical dilemmas. Indeed, it might be reassuring to wave that rule book in the face of the supervisor who suggests that a few well-placed gifts to local journalists might be appropriate. But this approach has limitations.

First, there can never be enough rules to cover everything that you might see as a moral dilemma. For every place and every time of your life there will be another set of circumstances and there may be no rule in your rule book to deal with this.

The second problem has to do with loopholes. What happens when people are faced with a series of rules such as those required by governments when you are completing your income tax return? The more rules there are, the more exceptions have to be made and this leads to a whole branch of ethical decision-making based on the search to discover loopholes.

The third problem is that rules are clearly open to interpretation. On the surface, a belief in a duty to be honest may appear simple to apply in the field of public relations. However, the way one person interprets the rule about honesty may be quite different from how another one does. For example, whereas they may both agree that to include a bold-faced lie in a media release would be highly unethical, they might disagree vehemently about whether it is necessary to include every detail so as to avoid any possibility of misleading the public.

And, of course, just as it is the case that one person's rights may conflict with another's as we discussed earlier, it is possible for one rule to conflict with another in a particular situation. For example, if there is one rule to avoid telling lies and another to avoid harming people, what do you do in a situation where to tell the complete truth to the media about what's going on with your client would harm one or more people? You may have rules to follow, but you still have a dilemma.

'SITUATIONS ALTER CASES'

I wonder if you noticed that several times throughout the preceding section on rule-based ethics, the word 'situation' came up. As hard as I tried to avoid it, it was usually the best word to use. I tried to avoid it because its very use seems to suggest somehow that you cannot get away from the circumstances of a situation when making ethical decisions and these kinds of considerations fall into the second category of ethical thinking.

When I was a young girl, my mother used to say this to me whenever I'd implore her to let me do something that she had clearly, at least in my mind, allowed my older sister to do. 'Situations alter cases', she'd say, comfortable in her ability to mete out fair decisions for her growing daughters.

My mother was demonstrating in her own way another basic approach to ethical decision-making: *situational ethics*. As the name implies, this approach allows for consideration of the special circumstances inherent in each situation, while still using fundamental principles as guidelines.

Using our example from above of conflicting rules, your company may have an open news policy and consider full disclosure of the facts to be the most ethical way to deal with media relations. From time to time, however, it may be in the best interests of one or more of the parties involved – the community, an employee, a client – to withhold details that could have damaging effects.

Situational ethics as a way of thinking about moral dilemmas was championed in the 1960s by an episcopal priest named Joseph Fletcher. His model is based on the notion that love is the only universal law and that decisions should be based on the circumstances of a particular situation. No fixed rule or law would supersede the assessment of the context. Whereas this is a religious-based approach to situational ethics with its reference to love, it isn't really any different from a more secular version that has been espoused through history by those who believe in the concept of moral relativism, which holds that there are no absolutes when it comes to ethics.

MORAL RELATIVISM AND SITUATIONS

Although moral relativism and situational ethical decision-making are not exactly the same thing, they are related and we need to explore this before we examine the problems associated with the situational approach.

Moral relativism is that philosophical approach that suggests that morality is largely culturally, historically and/or individually based. It contends that there are, in fact, no absolute rights and wrongs. Philosophy professor Wilfred Waluchow defines moral relativism as 'a view which rejects the notion that there is one, universally valid morality which can be discovered by moral reasoning'.[1]

For example, whereas in North America it is considered highly unethical to give gifts to journalists – or for journalists to accept them from PR practitioners for that matter – to secure favourable publicity, in other parts of the world it is common, accepted and even expected. Are those who bribe or are bribed in this context morally inferior to those of us who would not consider such a practice? Adherents of moral relativism would say 'no'. However, a public relations practitioner or journalist in North America who does the same thing would be considered by colleagues and likely the public to have committed an ethical transgression. And indeed, there is a current move in the industry to establish global guidelines, an approach that has both its supporters and its detractors.

It is often difficult for us to accept this concept when we have strong beliefs in our own cultural norms. But it does point out to us the difficulties in attempting to elucidate absolute rights and wrongs on the one hand, and taking a situational view of the circumstances on the other.

THE PROBLEM WITH SITUATIONS

Clearly, weighing all possible circumstances and their sequellae requires a significant amount of judgement on the part of the individual charged with making the final decision. Therein lies one of the main problems with the situational approach to making ethical decisions. The judgement capabilities of those charged with making ethical decisions can vary considerably. Not everyone has the same capability to reason things out in such a systematic and ultimately defensible way. Then, of course, since someone is making the decision, there is an opportunity for the less moral among us to abuse that power.

Another oft-mentioned problem with this approach is the clear possibility that because of the belief that circumstances alter cases, there is more possibility that decisions will be unfair. If your organization has a particular policy and uses a situational approach to apply it, there may come charges of unfair practice from those who do not like the decision made in their cases.

Although there are clearly drawbacks to both approaches, in a close examination of them in the context of making everyday ethical decisions in a field like public relations that deals with such disparate groups of people, a situational approach seems to have a wider appeal. The dogmatic approach of the rule-based devotees seems to run counter to the culture of the field.

In any case, because such a degree of judgement seems to be required in applying a situational approach, there is a clear need for ethics education for all public relations practitioners as one key to ensuring that when the time comes to make such an important judgement, your background and experience allow you to make a decision that is at least morally defensible, even if not everyone agrees with you (which is generally the case).

Note

1.   Waluchow, W (2003) *The Dimensions of Ethics: An introduction to ethical theory*, Broadview Press, Peterborough, ON, p 67

6

Robin Hood ethics

Do not do an immoral thing for moral reasons.

Thomas Hardy

Robin Hood was a utilitarian ethicist – or perhaps more accurately, he justified his actions by using utilitarian principles. In case you've forgotten, Robin Hood stole from the rich (stealing in general is and was considered immoral, never mind illegal), to give to the poor (what kind of knave would consider giving to the poor to be anything but good?). There is much that public relations practitioners could learn from delving further into the morality of Robin Hood's decision. It might come in handy.

Indeed, perhaps Edward Bernays was calling upon the ethical principle of utility when, in response to the mid-20th-century, post-war doom and gloom, he is reputed to have said 'The conscious and intelligent manipulation of the organized habits and opinions of the masses is an important element in a democratic society.' Others might consider this kind of statement to indicate that he was an elitist pimp rather than simply a man who saw that the end justified the means in this case. This brings us to the focus of this chapter: the usefulness of the principle of utility as a guiding precept in making ethical decisions in public relations. Although this book does not purport to present an exhaustive survey of philosophical underpinnings, the principle of utility has become so ubiquitous, often spuriously so, as a rationale for questionable actions in our society that it warrants a closer examination by public relations.

WHAT THE HECK IS 'UTILITARIANISM'?

When faced with what appears to be a moral dilemma, we often look to the philosophers who have examined good and evil, the moral and the immoral, in considerable detail through the years. Indeed, as long as there have been thinkers, there have been guiding principles. The concept of 'utilitarianism' is one such principle that is often used as a rationale for behaviour that needs to be justified. We begin our discussion by determining what utilitarianism is and how the concept developed.

The genesis of utilitarian ethics is generally attributed to 18th-century Englishman Jeremy Bentham, but perhaps the best known of the utilitarian ethicists is English philosopher John Stuart Mill, who augmented the concept in his book *Utilitarianism*. In a nutshell, this approach to ethical thinking takes the position that the rightness or wrongness of any action is dependent entirely on the outcomes that derive from it. In other words, neither the intent behind the action nor the fundamental rightness or wrongness of the action is at issue, only the consequences. This is a very pragmatic approach to ethical decision-making. Some kind of rational estimation of the outcome is made and the action is taken to maximize the greatest good (although Mill described it as 'happiness') for the greatest number of people. Of course, in most people's minds, this approach often results in the position that the end justifies the means.

Ethics writers Claire Andre and Manuel Velasquez put it this way: 'So long as a course of action produces maximum benefits for everyone, utilitarianism does not care whether the benefits are produced by lies, manipulation, or coercion.'[1] If you consider their further contention that we tend to use this way of ethical rationalization frequently in our daily lives, it seems that perhaps we ought to be looking beyond this principle. Is there, however, anything fundamentally wrong with this way of thinking?

If, in general, you believe that in public relations it is obligatory to tell the truth, could there be times when telling a falsehood might result in a better end for a greater number of people? Certainly, in times of war, for example, it might be considered in the best interests of the safety of large numbers of people to tell a lie to the media during a press conference.

It seems, then, that the principle might be a useful way to distribute the greatest good to the greatest number, if and only if the decision-makers are able to make an accurate judgement about the potential outcomes and that those outcomes go beyond the self-interest of those making the moral choice.

MOTIVES BE DAMNED

Many public relations approaches have the appearance of being utilitarian in nature. Consider the following case in light of its utilitarian aspects.

A quarter of a century ago, a certain (very large) international public relations firm took on the Argentine government as a client. During the late 1970s, Argentina was not a nice place to live if you were opposed in any way to the government. A military junta had seized power in 1976. It has been reported that in the first eight months after the coup, Amnesty International conducted an investigation and figured out that thousands of people were being held as political prisoners and that torture was routine and pervasive. This was President Rafael Videla's creation and the situation that existed when his government's Ministry of the Economy hired a certain North American-based PR firm to stimulate investment in this country whose reputation had, not surprisingly, begun to falter in the eyes of the world. In other words, they needed to shine up the image so that Argentina could borrow money on the world markets and sell their products. Using standard, modern North American ethical standards, is there any way to justify taking on such a client?

Yes, there is. That does not make it right or wrong, it just makes it justifiable – and here's how.

Arguably an oversimplification, but if we define the principle of utility by saying that you ought to strive for the greatest good for the greatest number, and further, that the end justifies the means, there is a moral rationale for the decision to represent this client. The PR agency could quite justifiably suggest that by representing this government, which seemed to represent evil incarnate, at least to many people throughout the world, and many of whose policies were counter to what we believe to be 'right' in terms of human rights, their work in supporting economic growth might, in the long term, be the greater good for the greatest number of people. It might help to get those begging children off the streets by putting their families to work, for example. Indeed, for a utilitarian ethicist, the motivation behind any particular decision is not what's important – only the outcome. If the PR agency in our case decided to take the case mostly for the money, justifying representation of the client by suggesting the good that will come, then they're off the hook – at least to other utilitarians. Their motives would not be questioned in the strict application of this principle, even if they were purely selfish. The general outcomes would balance this self-interest. It's not quite that simple, though.

Just as with the singular application of any ethical principle on its own, the application of this principle of utility has problems as well. Make no mistake, during Mill's life and even now, although his principle is included in probably every ethics text you might read, his views have been attacked again and again.

PROBLEMS WITH ROBIN HOOD

Here are some of the problems with its application to our situation. Somewhere along the line, someone has to be able to assess accurately the actual consequences, and that's a very tough call, especially when it comes to the outcomes of public relations campaigns. Ask anyone who does PR research. As much as we try to develop outcome objectives for our campaigns and then evaluate our success against these, outcomes in public communication are still dependent on so many variables over which we have no control. Unplanned outcomes are a fact of life in a field like public relations. Our work involves people and their attitudes and behaviours. In spite of the best research and plans based on knowledge of all the social science theories in the world, people are still frequently unpredictable – so too are mitigating circumstances outside our control. Public relations does not happen in a laboratory.

Perhaps even more worrisome, however, is the utilitarian notion that a society is a collection of individuals, and that what is good for these individuals can be added up to the public good, regardless of the atrocities being committed against any seemingly small segment. One of the basic tenets of ethics, as we have already determined, is to do no harm. Can the known harm be outweighed by the unknown outcomes – the unplanned results?

Perhaps we can learn something from the often vilified author-philosopher Ayn Rand, whose ethical theory of objectivism and its concept of rational self-interest have been the core of many ethical debates since she first published her best-selling novels *The Fountainhead* and *Atlas Shrugged* in the middle of the 20th century. She had this to say about this kind of approach to making moral judgements:

> When the 'common good' of a society is regarded as something apart from and superior to the individual good of its members, it means that the good of some men takes precedence over the good of others, with those others consigned to the status of sacrificial animals.[2]

So, sometimes you can do the right things for all the wrong reasons, but often the right thing is still ethically dubious. Robin Hood had no more claim to the moral high ground than a public relations practitioner working to support the aims of an ethically questionable client. When we move on to our discussion of the ethics of specific public relations approaches in Part 3, we'll discuss in more depth the morality of applying these techniques to clients whose ethics have been questioned.

Notes

1. Andre, Claire and Velasquez, Manuel [accessed 25 September 2003] Calculating the consequences: the utilitarian approach to ethics, *Issues in Ethics*, **2** (1), Winter, 1989.　http://www.scu.edu/ethics/publications/iie/v2n1/calculating.html
2. Rand, A (1966) What is capitalism? In *Capitalism: The unknown ideal*, The New American Library, Inc, New York

Part 2

Ethics and the practitioner

Now that we have examined some aspects of an ethical framework that lies beneath the real, everyday issues, we need to look at you, the person and public relations practitioner – at the personal aspects of ethical decision-making that underlie those professional decisions.

Sometimes taking a good, close look at who we are as moral individuals can be a very eye-opening experience. Everything from how evolved we are, morally speaking, to our level of respect for others as manifested in our manners, is a part of our personal ethics. Then, of course, there is the matter of how we react to ethical standards expected of us by our profession.

You are faced with those professional codes of ethics, but what are you really supposed to do with them? You know, on a gut level, what decision you'd make in hypothetical ethical dilemmas, but do you know what your decisions say to the world about you as a moral person? And what about conflicts? Do you even recognize when you as an individual are facing a conflict of interest in your work situation? Many people don't. How do you handle specific crises of conscience?

Part 2 is designed to help you to answer these questions for yourself.

7

Your staircase to respect

Good character is more to be praised than outstanding talent. Most talents are, to some extent, a gift. Good character, by contrast, is not given to us. We have to build it piece by piece – by thought, choice, courage and determination.

John Luther

What does it mean to respect others? We talk about it all the time as if it were truly something laudable. However, viewing the nightly news each evening might lead us to the defensible conclusion that there is an epidemic of disrespect for others going on in our world today. But make no mistake about it, respect for others is the foundation for an individual's ability to function in an ethical way – whether we're talking about respect for people or the environment for that matter.

R-E-S-P-E-C-T

Even soul star Aretha Franklin sang for it when all she was asking for was 'a little respect'. Rodney Dangerfield has relied on his line that he can't get

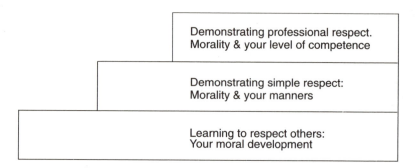

Figure 7.1 *The staircase to respect*

any. All they were asking for was to be treated with consideration, for their human qualities to be held in high regard. If we turn that search for respect around and consider what it means to give respect to others, it seems clear that without respect, it might be difficult or even impossible to make defensible ethical decisions. Without being able to respect our colleagues, clients, employers, members of the community, the media and so on, the ethical foundation for the development of trusting relationships would crumble, just as it does for us on a personal basis.

In this discussion of respect, we'll examine three levels of respect that might provide each of us as individual PR practitioners with a foundation for demonstrating respect as the basis for our ethical behaviour. Figure 7.1 illustrates the three steps on the staircase to respect. The bottom step is understanding how we develop an ability to respect others, and by examining our own development we begin to understand our own level of moral maturity. Taking the second step, we focus on simple measures of respect for others on an interpersonal level: the relationship between morality and manners. On the final step on our staircase (this is not an exhaustive description of all aspects of respect), we'll examine an example of one important way that you demonstrate professional respect for employers, clients, your profession and society by discussing ethical issues related to your level of professional competence.

STILL THE MORAL CHILD

Consider the following scenario. Julia has been working for a large, national public relations and marketing firm since she received her PR degree five years ago. She considers herself to be a 'go-getter'. 'Driven' is how most of her friends from university put it. For five years she's worked 60 to 80 hours a week and pulled her share of all-nighters to meet those deadlines. Although she has found it exhilarating and somewhat rewarding, she doesn't believe she has been rewarded quite fast enough. In fact, she's looking for a way to get that promotion and rise that seem to have eluded her for the past year or two.

But a new client's file has just landed on her desk and she knows how she can solve their public relations problem and come out looking like a creative genius. There's only one catch. The solution she knows will work involves using a bit of information that she gleaned while working on a communication audit for one of the new client's competitors.

After work on Friday, Julia meets two of her old friends from university for a drink at a downtown bar. While they're happily sequestered in a private booth, sipping Martinis, Julia casually mentions her genius idea for her new client.

'You can't do that', says one friend, the PR director of a small IT company. 'It's wrong.'

'I agree', says the other friend, a media relations consultant. 'What would you do if you got caught?'

It seems that Julia's friends, both in the same field as she is, are in agreement: using that piece of proprietary information for her own gain, or even the gain of a client, shouldn't be done. Are they right? Their answers might be the same, but their motivations for them are quite different. Is one of these friends more right than the other? The answer depends upon how important it is to you to do the right thing for the right reasons. And the reasons we act ethically depend largely on the level of moral development that we are demonstrating at that point, limited by the extent to which we have developed at all.

THE MORAL CHILD GROWS UP

Moral development refers to the way in which we as individuals formulate a sense of morality as we develop as human beings. We aren't born with the ability to think in an ethical manner: a baby cries for attention when he or she needs something and it is irrelevant to that baby if someone else has needs. The baby is unaware of others. As young children, our worlds begin to expand to include our families and others who come into our immediate world. Eventually, as fully developed adults we have the capacity to consider others whose lives may never even touch ours directly.

American psychologist Lawrence Kohlberg, who did most of his work in the 1960s, examined children's responses to ethical dilemmas and developed a theory about how we develop as moral individuals. Figure 7.2 summarizes his descriptions of three levels and six stages of moral development.

Kohlberg's stages of Moral Development
(Your reasons for doing what's 'right')

Level I: The pre-conventional level
- Stage 1:... to avoid punishment
- Stage 2:... to serve your own needs

Level II: The conventional level
- Stage 3:... to be a good person in your eyes and the eyes of others
- Stage 4:... to fulfil duties to which you have agreed to keep the system running

Level III: The Post-conventional level
- Stage 5:... to fulfil a social contract or do what has the highest degree of utility
- Stage 6:... to follow a self-chosen set of universal ethical principles

Figure 7.2   *Kohlberg's stages of moral development (your reasons for doing what's 'right')*

His theory suggests that we as individuals first learn to satisfy our own needs: at an early stage of our development as young children we do what's right to avoid punishment or simply to serve our own needs. For example, a child is told it's wrong to steal and quickly learns that he or she will be punished if caught. In this child's mind, stealing isn't inherently wrong – they haven't learned that yet, if they ever do. It only results in punishment; thus they avoid stealing to avoid punishment. At the next stage, they might do what's right only if there is something in it for them. Our prisons are populated by people who have never really progressed beyond this level of moral reasoning.

Kohlberg says that eventually, most, but not all, people move into a more conventional level where they are able to consider not only themselves, but also a widening circle of other people. This seems to be the stage at which most adults function. At this stage, you might do what's right because you want others to think of you as a good person or to fulfil duties that you have agreed upon to keep the system running. For example, if your organization has a code of ethics, whereas you might not truly believe in or care about one or more of the tenets, you behave in a manner that supports the code because you've agreed to do so by signing a contract.

People who reach the highest levels of development are those who are able to take a genuine interest in the welfare of others and develop a sense of morality that allows them to follow a self-chosen set of universal ethical principles. Kohlberg, however, doesn't believe that many adults ever truly reach this level of moral functioning.

(To satisfy those who are aware of the criticisms of Kohlberg's theory, I am well aware that it was based on research with Anglo-American teenaged boys and that subsequent applications of his research methods to girls had slightly different results. However, I think that there is still much we can learn from his theory, especially in examining our own motives for making ethical decisions.)

If we consider Julia's dilemma in this context, it seems clear that if she decides to follow through with her plan, she would be acting unethically. But, perhaps even more important from an ethical point of view, if she chooses not to follow through only because she feels she might get caught, she still isn't acting with integrity – she's doing it for the wrong reason. Like a morally undeveloped young child, she is acting morally only to avoid punishment. What will happen the next time she's faced with a similar dilemma? If she thinks she can get away with it – because no one is looking – she may feel justified in acting immorally. As you might have figured out by now, this is in direct contrast to a kind of decision-making based on the principle of utility that eschews motives for outcomes. Clearly, however, in this case, one could only say that the potential good outcome would be strictly for Julia herself – hardly the greatest good for the greatest number!

Next, we'll apply this knowledge of developmental stages of morality to a situation that every PR practitioner might find himself or herself in and might not even be aware of the issues.

AN ETHICAL LITMUS TEST?

You may have learnt about them in university or college, or you may have had to learn by trial and error. However you came to the knowledge and skills, every one of you who has ever applied for a job has one – a resumé, that is. You may call it a curriculum vitae (as long-winded academics like to – I have one), a work history or simply a resumé, but whether you like it or not, it speaks volumes about you – and not just about your work-related knowledge and skills. It also provides the reader with a snapshot of your moral character, although he or she may not find out the truth until later, perhaps until it is too late.

Puffing up the resumé

About five years ago, I received an e-mail from a former student who had, after some difficulty, found what he considered to be a terrific PR job halfway across the country. He proudly attached a copy of the press release announcing his appointment. The information it contained was created by his company based on the work history he had detailed in his resumé, presumably one of the reasons they hired him at all. To say I was surprised by its content was an understatement.

There in black and white on my computer screen was a description of someone I did not seem to know at all. The person depicted in the news release had experience with developing and implementing public relations plans and media relations strategies for several well-known companies, and seemed to have had a progressively successful career of at least five to seven years, although that specific detail was absent. What I did know was that this young man had graduated only a year earlier and that he had spent the previous year working in a completely unrelated field. Yet there was something familiar about the work history.

After some thinking, I finally figured it out. He had, indeed, worked for the companies mentioned and had even 'participated in' each of the activities described. The problem was that he had done this while on individual four-month work terms while a student in our programme and under the supervision of both faculty and employers. There was nothing in the press release to suggest that he had been anything short of the lead PR counsel for these organizations. And of course, resumés never do indicate that as a student he was less than stellar – something else I, as one of his former professors, knew only too well.

I call this a 'puffed-up' resumé. Its content is based on a slim slice of the truth which subsequently puffs like the puffed crust of one of those pizzas with the obscenely fat edges.

What was particularly interesting about this young man was that he was sending this piece to me, someone who knew the truth about his experience. It was difficult to determine if he was just plain stupid or if he really thought it was fine to do this. Clearly, he never considered that he might get found out.

Another particular temptation to public relations practitioners is related to their particular expertise. PR people, with their considerable writing talents, can make even the most mundane job seem sublimely important when they are creating their resumés. Indeed, I've seen my share of this kind of resumé puffery. But it is not the only way to demonstrate your level of moral development in resumé rookery.

Padding the resumé

Unlike puffing the resumé, in my definition padding is adding patently false information that isn't based on any grain of truth.

In a January 2003 issue of *Business Week* magazine, a small piece tells of three executives who had padded their resumés with fake degrees.[1] It seems that the board of a large software company discovered that their chief financial officer never did graduate from Stanford University's business school and no one had noticed for some 15 years. In another situation, evidently the chairman and CEO of Bausch and Lomb Inc falsely claimed to have an MBA from New York University. This falsehood cost him a bonus of $1.1 million. In another case, the head of MCG Capital Corp. admitted that he had never received the undergraduate degree on his resumé.

You might say, what's the difference now? These people have been able to fulfil the requirements of their jobs successfully for many years. They clearly did their jobs well for some years. That, however, is not the point. The point is the level of moral thinking that these resumé problems represent.

If these high-powered, high-profile individuals padded their resumés with credentials they did not possess, how many others in more lowly positions are doing the same thing? And why did they do it? Well, at least part of that answer is clear: because they didn't think they'd get caught – and for a long time, they were right. Which brings us to the issue of what such padding and puffing says about the person who does it.

First, it appears that these individuals are functioning at a relatively low level of moral development: they choose to do something questionable, thinking that they are unlikely to get caught. One can infer from this way of thinking that they would make what we might consider to be the moral choice only in circumstances where they knew that they might otherwise get caught or when there was something in it for them.

Second, and perhaps even more pervasive, is what this behaviour says about their level of respect for those who are reading their resumés.

As illustrated in the *Business Week* article cases, sometimes the dishonesty in the padding isn't recognized until some time later. Indeed, these individuals probably thought they were home free – that they would not get caught. What does this say for their level of respect for those hiring them? Demonstrating a low level of moral reasoning often indicates a low level of consideration for others. It is this consideration of others that is further demonstrated in interpersonal interactions – simple good manners, or lack thereof.

MORE THAN GOOD MANNERS: ETHICS AND ETIQUETTE

As parents, we use every device at our disposal to encourage 'polite' behaviour in our young children. Surely one of our objectives is to raise citizens whose behaviour reflects basic respect for others. Attempting to 'do the right thing' while being singularly unable to treat others with consideration is likely to lead to ethical decisions that reflect an inhumane approach.

If you take a walk through one of your local big-box bookstores, you might conclude that we are currently experiencing a veritable renaissance of etiquette consciousness. Business moguls have arisen to take up the battle cry. Good manners mean good business.

Do you consider yourself to be polite? Are you well-mannered? Are you respectful of others no matter what their place? Are you ethical? Perhaps we need to stop here. What *is* the relationship between ethics and etiquette?

Similar definitions

If we examine the dictionary definitions of ethics and etiquette, we see striking similarities. Funk and Wagnall's defines etiquette as 'rules conventionally established for behavior in polite society or official or professional life'.[2] Removal of the words 'polite society' results in a definition of ethics that resembles those frequently seen in textbooks. Indeed, another dictionary provides one definition of etiquette as '... the code of ethical behavior [sic] regarding professional practice or action among the members of a profession in their dealings with each other'.[3]

Codes of ethics, as set down by professional associations such as the Chartered Institute of Public Relations, are really nothing more than conventions for behaviour in applying moral standards to practical dilemmas.

Years ago, when I first began reading about business etiquette, I came upon what one writer suggested as the most important rule: *Everyone is important*. Basic respect for everyone – your secretary, the courier, the co-op student, the designer, the client, your boss, the janitor – both smoothes working relationships and assists in the more formidable task of making good ethical decisions. Besides, Emerson said, 'It is a rule of manners to avoid exaggeration.' As a rule of etiquette in public relations, it might be one worth our consideration.

How are your manners?

Since etiquette is concerned with correct or appropriate behaviour in personal as well as business situations and has, at its root, respect for others, it seems that possessing good manners is a key part of being able to behave in an acceptable manner. And we certainly expect that individuals learn manners from direct instruction by parents and teachers, personal observation of others and trial and error. But many people are still unsure of themselves. So, how are *your* manners, anyway?

Figure 7.3 provides a series of questions for you to consider as they apply to you. They don't refer to specific situations of specific etiquette such as how to introduce people and which fork to use for your starter when dining out. For those you'll have to refer to a comprehensive etiquette guide (and I'd strongly recommend that you do so). This test refers more to general areas of respect for others that are evidenced by your manners.

Test your manners

1. Do you always say please and thank you even when the person is 'just doing his or her job'?
2. Are you always careful to especially acknowledge when someone goes out of his or her way for you? If you cannot do it at the time, do you remember to do it later?
3. Do you always seek privacy for unpleasant encounters?
4. Do you always control your temper?
5. Do you refrain from using profane or rude language even when under pressure and even in business e-mail?
6. Do you refrain from making sexist or ethnic remarks or forwarding jokes that contain either?
7. Do you refer to others with the degree of formality that you expect to receive?

[Adapted from A Parsons and P Parsons (1992), *Health Care Ethics*, Toronto: Wall and Emerson.]

If you answered **NO** to any of these questions, you need to re-examine your basic manners and do something about it!

Figure 7.3 *Test your manners*

Perhaps Fred Astaire was right when he said 'The hardest job kids face today is learning good manners without seeing any.' If your manners are not what should be seen by children, you might want to do a bit of soul-searching before you even consider the next step in our staircase to respect: demonstrating professional respect for others.

MORALITY AND YOUR LEVEL OF COMPETENCE

Respecting our clients, our communities and ourselves requires us to exhibit competence in our professional activities. The Code of Professional Standards of the Canadian Public Relations Society says surprisingly little about it, as does the IABC Code. The Public Relations Society of America's Code of Ethics is only slightly more concerned about it. Can we conclude from the lack of discussion about the issue of competence in public relations that there are few ethical concerns about it? Or, rather, is it more likely that the issue of competence is a difficult one to measure and therefore an unpopular issue about which to provide ethical guidelines?

The truth is that as a profession, we provide a service to society. In doing so, society has a right to expect a certain level of competence in your ability to actually do your job. Indeed, would you consider it ethical for a doctor to practise medicine if he or she did not possess the required level of competence as measured by performance on the licensing examinations? When a doctor hangs out his or her shingle, you the patient infer from it the message 'I'm a competent physician. You can trust me.' Nothing less should be expected from a PR practitioner who sets up shop or goes to work for an organization. Anything less than professional competence to do your job could surely be seen at the very least as lying.

The questions: How can you ensure that your level of competence in the practice of public relations fulfils your responsibilities to society when we are not required to achieve a standard like one that might be imposed by a licensing board? How can we demonstrate our professional respect by ensuring that we maintain an acceptable level of professional competence?

Help from the professional codes?

We often look to professional codes of ethics to help us begin our search for answers to ethical dilemmas, recognizing that whereas we might find a direction, we do not expect to find the final answer. The Canadian Public Relations Society code says 'A member shall not guarantee specified results beyond the member's capacity to achieve.'[4] The International Association of Business Communicators indicates a sentiment that is almost identical, while the Public Relations Society of America is somewhat more direct about the issue. In their introductory list of values upon which the tenets of the code are based, they identify *expertise* and explain what they mean this way: 'We acquire and responsibly use specialized knowledge and experience. We advance the profession through continued professional development, research, and education. We build mutual understanding, credibility, and relationships among a wide array of institutions and audiences.'[5] Then, in their provisions of the code itself they indicate that members should 'actively pursue personal professional development'.

The Global Ethics Protocol as suggested by the Global Alliance for Public Relations and Communication Management proposes 'expertise' as one of its protocol standards and says this:

> We will encourage members to acquire and responsibly use specialized knowledge and experience to build understanding and client/employer credibility. Furthermore we will actively promote and advance the profession through continued professional development, research, and education.[6]

Thus, it appears that whereas competence is something of interest to the ethical public relations practitioner and that it is, indeed, an ethical concern, we still cannot answer the question about how to ensure your level of competence. The codes tell us that it is important – and thus we can connect it directly to our ethical responsibilities – but no one seems to be able to define precisely what that competency might consist of.

The true meaning of competence

The codes of ethics seem to shy away from actually using the word *competence*, instead selecting words such as expertise, knowledge and experience (CPRS avoids specific words entirely).

With all the talk today about incompetence and how it is to be avoided at all costs in any field (indeed, haven't we all observed PR behaviour that we labelled incompetent?), it seems more than germane to the issue to define the term competence. One useful definition of the term is 'possession of required skill, knowledge, qualification, or capacity'.[7] Our problem in the field of public relations is that *there are no required skills, knowledge or qualifications*. Anyone who pleases can print up business cards and go into business. It is specifically this area of a lack of requirements to enter into the practice of public relations that leads to problems in identifying and, more importantly, doing something about incompetence.

In 2007, the ethnographer Dr Rita Devine, along with students at Ryerson University in Toronto, examined the competencies exhibited by winning submissions to the awards programme of the Canadian Public Relations Society. Making the assumption that these would be exemplars – and indeed they are often presented as such as teaching cases in educational programmes – these young researchers were surprised and disappointed to discover something quite different.

They found that even these winning strategists 'often confused goals with objectives and objectives with strategies' and often failed to identify well-developed, measurable objectives, surely basic competencies expected of professional PR practitioners. In the end she concludes 'Some were simply written without the sophistication expected of professionally-produced plans… [A] few did not even appear to be proof-read.'[8] This provides us with a startling commentary and starkly realistic, albeit anecdotal example of the lack of professional standards regarding competence in our field.

In a professional sense, there are two main objectives to achieving competence in the field. In public relations the primary one is to protect the public. One need only read books like Sheldon Rampton and John Stauber's books *Toxic Sludge is Good for You* and *Trust Us, We're Experts* to understand the potential for harm to the public when public relations uses its power without concern for the harm it might cause. The second objective of ensuring competence is to secure the future of PR's image as an ethical pursuit. But, there are few external measures of competence. (Keep in mind that even if you graduated from a public relations degree or diploma programme, it doesn't mean that your level of competence will always be appropriate.)

Competence to practise, then, becomes more of a personal commitment to professional excellence and one way that you can clearly demonstrate your respect for your clients and employers, your profession and society.

Your ethical responsibility to be competent

You owe it to yourself, to your employers and clients, to your profession and to society to be competent to act in the capacity of a public relations practitioner (see Figure 7.4).

Public relations competence checklist

Consider the following statements as a guide to reflecting on your personal level of competence in the practice of public relations.

☐ I consider my educational background to be appropriate to my current public relations position.
☐ I rarely have to define my credentials to my peers.
☐ I read the PR industry literature regularly both in print and on line.
☐ I attend professional development sessions on an annual basis.
☐ I recognize when I am facing situations for which I am ill-prepared.
☐ I have a public relations mentor (for early careerists).
☐ I am a mentor to a young practitioner (for later careerists).
☐ I have a network of colleagues with whom I can consult on PR-related issues.
☐ I have plans to enhance my educational preparation as a move forward in my career.

Figure 7.4 *Public relations competence checklist*

While we all recognize that not all of us have the same levels of skills regardless of our educational background, our responsibility to be competent has three components:

1. to ensure that we have the skills necessary to do the work that we take on at any given time;
2. to ensure that we avoid giving employers or clients the impression that we can guarantee specific results; and
3. to keep our knowledge, skills and expertise current.

The question remains: How do you accomplish this? Here are some ideas:

1. Take a formal course from a local college or university. Even universities that do not offer specific programmes in public relations often offer courses that are closely related in terms of both background and skills. Don't be fooled into thinking that the only kinds of courses you need are skill-related. As you develop your career, more than ever you need to consider educational cross-training. Consider courses in cultural studies, conflict management, philosophy, applied science. In fact, try any kind of course that forces you to think about the world in a different way. It can bring freshness to your work in PR.
2. Attend professional development (PD) sessions. Since PR is largely an urban profession, most PR practitioners have access to regular PD sessions sponsored by professional associations. And try to get to a national or international conference once in a while.
3. Consider teaching a PD session or a course yourself. It is often said that teaching is one of the best ways of learning (and I'll vouch for that). Whereas you will certainly teach something that you know a lot about, you'll also learn a lot, and students' questions (generally the ones for which you don't have ready answers) can lead you to learn more about areas that you hadn't previously considered.
4. Read, read, read. Read PR and industry-related magazines, journals and books, but also read material that isn't directly related to PR. Cross-reading is considered to be a very useful way to kick-start your creative thought processes.
5. Consider obtaining a recognized PR credential. Professional associations have such programmes which bring us ever closer to the notion of actually being able to measure competence (at least at the time you went through the accreditation process).

Throughout history, PR has been sprinkled with practitioner after practitioner whom we would now consider to lack the necessary competence to practise ethical public relations. Let's make this just an historical blip and not a prediction for the future.

THE VIRTUE OF HUMILITY

In Chapter 3 we discussed the concept of virtue ethics; at this point we have established that respecting others is a fundamental part of ethical behaviour. Could there be a relationship between the two? I believe so, and one of the so-called virtues that speaks directly to that issue is humility. It deserves some consideration in any discussion of you as an individual.

It might be too much of a stretch for you to even consider the term *public relations practitioner* in the same sentence with the word *humility*. It might cause too much cognitive dissonance! But let's stretch our minds for a few minutes and talk about it. Is there any ethical virtue in humility and how might it be a useful frame through which we might view our work? The bottom line is this: could you do your work better if you acted with a higher degree of humility?

What exactly is humility? The term is generally defined as the quality of being humble, which isn't very useful if you don't know what it means to be humble. You might begin by thinking about anyone you know who happens to fit the following description: arrogant, conceited, prideful. Then think of the opposite. I am not referring, however, to someone who is weak, exhibits self-loathing or false modesty, or who is falsely self-effacing. Think, rather of a Mother Theresa type: someone clear about her place in the world, determined to achieve her objectives and yet intimidated by public praise. She was a good example of the personification of humility.

How many colleagues do you know who appear to share very much in common with Mother Theresa? Perhaps you have a different circle of peers, but I have yet to meet very many in our field: among my own colleagues in my home town, at conferences attended by practitioners farther afield or – although I'm hesitant to even bring it up – among my students who are the future of the field. On those rare occasions when I note a public relations practitioner with a sense of personal humility I find these people to be generally older, more experienced in work and life, and very good at what they do. Overall, however, we're not a humble lot in this field, and perhaps that comes with the territory; but should we consider being more so? What would a little humility do to our field? And why might it contribute to ethical behaviour?

According to Charles Toftoy and Rena Jabbour, 'The most significant characteristic of humility is the ability for an individual to assume responsibility for shortcomings, rather than blaming them on such external factors as other underperforming employees or even sheer bad luck.'[9] They suggest that the individual who acts with habitual humility looks in the mirror, rather than out the window.

Consider two different reactions to the same situation. You are leader of a hard-working and very capable three-person team preparing for an important event to mark the opening of your new facilities. The non-profit organization for which you work has toiled long and hard for several years to raise the money. On the day of the event, your most important donor comes to you, knowing that you are in charge of the event and comments on how well-organized this event is and how much he appreciates your hard work. Do you smile, shake his hand and thank him, knowing that his approbation could stand you in good stead for the promotion you so dearly covet? Or do you say thank you and indicate to him that you could certainly not have done it without the teamwork exhibited by your colleagues?

What if, on that same day, one of your most generous donors comes to you to draw your attention to the fact that her name is misspelled on both the programme and the plaque at the door of the room that her money furnished. One of your team members was responsible for the final editing of all materials that went to the printer and to the plaque engravers. Do you mention to her that the team member who was responsible must have missed it and that you will take him to task? Or do you apologize and take responsibility for the mistake since it was ultimately *your* team?

Your reaction indicates a number of things about you – character traits that may not be visible to that donor at that time, but will surely have an impact on your future success.

A person who exhibits personal humility first and foremost takes responsibility for his or her work. If you are the team leader, then you are responsible not only for your own work but for that of the people to whom you have delegated. Does that mean that you continually flagellate yourself for both your own and others' mistakes? Certainly not. That would be a false sense of humility. You are simply accountable for your decisions and your actions.

A person who acts with humility is considerate of others and respects them. He or she is able to give credit to others when they are due the credit, and does not take the limelight without ensuring that all those who should be in it have their moment there. This person of humility is therefore open to the ideas of others, not always believing that his or her ideas are the only ones that are worthy of consideration. And according to Toftoy and Jabbour, this person acting with humility will always take the 'harder right' rather than the 'easier wrong'.[10]

Respecting others is fundamental to our ability to make good ethical decisions, so that means that if we are able to be somewhat modest, although not in a false way, we can develop a kind of dignity that respects both ourselves and others. From that respect comes trust and trustworthiness. What kind of person would you like to be and, perhaps even more telling, what kind of person would you prefer to work with?

In public relations we are often seen as the ones pushing our organizations or clients as well as ourselves, because promotion of ideas is the lifeblood of PR. This can be perceived as arrogance, self-importance or even conceit. We need to be committed to our issues and our causes, but this can be done much more effectively with a graciousness that is borne of honest humility.

Notes

1. Padded resumés, *Business Week*, 13 January 2003, Issue 3815, p 84
2. *Funk & Wagnall's Standard Desk Dictionary*, vol 1 (1975), Funk & Wagnall's, New York, p 218
3. Infoplease online dictionary [accessed 19 January 2003]. http://www.infoplease.com/ipd/A0429648.html
4. Canadian Public Relations Society [accessed 21 November 2003] *Code of Professional Standards.* http://www.cprs.ca/AboutCPRS/e_code.htm
5. Public Relations Society of America [accessed 21 November 2003] *Code of Ethics.* http://www.prsa.org/_About/ethics/preamble.asp?ident=eth3
6. Global Alliance for Public Relations and Communication Management [accessed 21 November 2003] *Global Protocol on Public Relations Ethics.* http://www.globalpr.org/knowedge/ethics/protocol.asp
7. Infoplease.com [accessed 21 November 2003] http://www.infoplease.com/ipd/A0382180.
8. Devine, Rita (2007) Rescuing PR's reputation, *Communication World*, July–August, p 36
9. Toftoy, Charles and Jabbour, Rena (2005) The lost entrepreneurial trait for success: the virtue of humility, *Electronic Journal of Business Ethics and Organizational Studies* [accessed 15/11/2005] http://ejbo.jyu.fi/index.cgi?page=articles/0901_7
10. Toftoy and Jabbour, Ibid

8

The good, the bad and the (almost) ugly: ethics codes

Good people do not need laws to tell them to act responsibly, while bad people will find a way around the laws.

Plato

Christians have the Ten Commandments, Buddhists have the Eightfold Path, adherents to just about any other formalized religion have a set of rules, a code if you like, to live by, and if you believe the fictionalized versions of organized crime, even the Mafia has a code of 'honour'. In the field of public relations we have these codes, too: codes of ethics by the hundreds.

The Center for the Study of Ethics in the Professions lists some 850 codes of ethics on its website.[1] If you draw any conclusion from this it might be that a whole lot of people have spent an inordinate amount of time considering ethical behaviour and making up rules – or at least guidelines – for moral behaviour. Most professional organizations have codes of ethics, and public relations and communications organizations are no different. The Chartered Institute of Public Relations, the International Association of Business Communicators, the Canadian Public Relations Society, the Public Relations Society of America and the International Public Relations Association, for example, all have their own codes. There has even been an attempt to produce a so-called global protocol for ethics in public relations. So, what is a code and what's so good (or bad) about it?

CODES AS CONTRACTS

Perhaps one of the most useful ways of looking at a code of ethics is as a profession's contract with the society it serves rather than, as some people may like to believe, a cookbook to thumb through when looking for the answer to a dilemma.

The preface to IABC's *Code of Ethics for Professional Communicators* sets up this contractual arrangement in this way:

> Because hundreds of thousands of business communicators worldwide engage in activities that affect the lives of millions of people, and because this power carries with it significant social responsibilities, the International Association of Business Communicators developed the Code...[2]

This statement sets up the expectation that practitioners of these communication disciplines will recognize their power to influence (their job) and will provide these services in a particular way (their promise). In this way they articulate a contractual arrangement of sorts with society. If you examine codes of ethics in this light, they seem to make a certain amount of sense. The code makes a kind of promise about what behaviour can be expected. But there is a fundamental lingering question here. Is this the least we can expect, or perhaps the most?

MINIMUM STANDARDS OR IDEALS?

The nagging question that always seems to haunt me when I read these various codes of ethics is this: are these guidelines for the minimum standard of acceptable behaviour below which a practitioner could presumably be censured by the organization, or are they merely a set of articulated ideals towards which we, as members of that organization, ought to strive, presumably falling short from time to time? It occurs to me that those members who have been engaged in developing these codes consider them to be the minimum standards; however, given the lack of teeth that the codes seem to have, they appear to the public to be nothing more than wishful thinking. There is a faint hope that perhaps members will strive to meet these lofty ideals. So arises the debate: do we really need these codes at all or are they simply window dressing?

WHO NEEDS CODES, ANYWAY?

Even if you think about a code of ethics as a kind of contract that sets out, in very general terms, acceptable moral behaviour, there is still considerable disagreement about whether professions (not just public relations and communication professions) ought to have codes at all.

The primary argument against the requirement for professional codes of ethics is the belief that there need not be any special code of ethics apart from the moral guidelines within a given society, for example the Ten Commandments in a Christian society. This position suggests that members of any specific profession are not special and different in any way from anyone else in society and therefore have no extraordinary duties, responsibilities or even rights. Try telling that to physicians who have been clinging to a higher code (at least in their own minds it is higher) since the time of Hippocrates.

Another argument against the value of professional codes of ethics takes the position that it is possible that some practitioners might interpret a code of ethics so literally as to think that this is all they need to make moral decisions – that this code is the extent to which they believe they ever need to think about ethics at all. This is a frightening thought, especially in light of our contention that perhaps these codes set out only minimum standards of acceptability. Minimally ethical practitioners crowding a field such as public relations hardly bode well for the continual improvement of ethical standards, especially given our spotty history and reputation.

It is this spotty history and less-than-spotless reputation that public relations holds within society that make some sceptics believe that our codes of ethics are nothing more than a PR exercise – one designed to impress those who say we have no ethics, yet completely unenforceable in any case.

A code of ethics is one of the ways by which sociologists (at least) decide whether or not a particular occupation is a formal 'profession' or not. Codes of ethics for public relations practitioners have been viewed by their critics as nothing more than an attempt to professionalize an unprofessional occupation.

Whereas there might be some substance to this commentary on our field of practice, the bottom line remains that a code of ethics at the very least provides a point of departure for discussions about what constitutes unethical behaviour in any field. It is probably true that if we had a collection of individuals whose own moral standards are high, we would need to worry less about creating codes, but since that is likely never to happen in PR or any other field, perhaps these codes might help to guide our discussion at least.

A GLOBAL CODE?

If there is controversy about the need for codes at all, despite the fact that there are plenty of them around, as we have already discussed, why would anyone want to create yet another one – a global code or protocol, as it is specifically named?

The Global Alliance for Public Relations and Communication Management is the most recent membership organization to weigh in on the issue of the advantages of a worldwide code of ethics, cultural differences notwithstanding. The code that was developed and floated at an international conference in 2003 is provided to the member associations as 'a yardstick by which [member associations are] to review and revise their own Code...[3] This will at least result in some consistency in ethics codes throughout the world.

The notion of a code of ethics that is consistent throughout the world implies that society, with whom we have a contract to provide a certain kind of specialized service, can expect a uniform level of moral behaviour that is considered to be acceptable within a peer group. However, whether it is a local code, a regional code, a national code or a global code, it can still suffer from the same limitations that we have already discussed. On the upside, few of us could argue with the conclusion that even sitting down as an international group and discussing ethical concerns is a valuable exercise – at least for those fortunate enough to have been members of the committee.

The unanswered question, however, still remains: is the field of public relations any more ethical because we have codes of ethics than it would be if we just forgot about them? Codes are a place to begin but not a place to end.

RELYING ON A PERSONAL CODE

By the time I had finished teaching our new stand-alone public relations ethics course to our third-year PR students, I was still perplexed about how to evaluate them. If a student knew a lot about ethics and yet made what I considered to be a morally reprehensible decision, did I have the right to make such a judgement and fail that student? On the other hand, what would I do with a student who seemed to have gleaned no knowledge about ethics and morality and yet when faced with a decision used his or her own personal values to make what I might deem a sound decision? And, anyway, who was I to be making these ethical pronouncements? Naturally, I had set objectives at the beginning for what the students would be expected to accomplish, and this should tell me what I must evaluate. But educational theory notwithstanding, I was still perplexed.

Let me state the question: Is it appropriate to measure the extent to which the students understand and can apply ethical theory to ethical decision-making in public relations practice? Or, should students be given marks based on their ability to make these decisions with a high level of integrity (as defined by the textbooks and me)? Should they be marked at all?

Figuring out how much students have learnt about the theory and the processes is relatively easy and probably tells me whether or not they met the educational objectives. But, if the reason we add courses on ethics to the basic public relations degree is to ensure that, in future, the field is practised with a high degree of integrity, wouldn't the second approach (evaluating the ability to make morally defensible decisions) provide a more appropriate basis for evaluation? Shouldn't the most 'ethical' students in the class who are able to function with the highest level of moral standards receive the highest grades? This is a real dilemma.

A case in point

Towards the end of the course, we began discussing specific public relations cases, trying to come to a consensus as a group about the best, most ethical ways of dealing with practical situations. One of the sources I used for these cases is the Public Relations Society of America's (PRSA's) Code of Ethics Case Study Series. Here's a summary of one of the cases we discussed in class:

> You're the PR director for a housing developer who is getting ready to market some lots to middle income families. The site is on a former land-fill and government reports show 'very low levels of contaminants that are not life-threatening'. You tell the boss how to handle this in the promotional materials and he says not to discuss it proactively at all. What to do?[4]

The in-class discussion was very interesting. PRSA discusses key values such as honesty, independence, loyalty and fairness as providing guidance in this situation, with a clear sense that these values might even conflict with one another. Students seemed to be able to come up with the same list. Part of the final PRSA solution goes like this: 'You must convince your boss that it is in the company's best interest to acknowledge the history of the land… The reputation of the company will be enhanced by proactive communications… Your reputation as a public relations practitioner depends on your skills to persuade your employer to act in the best interest of the public.' (For the complete discussion go to the PRSA website and look up Case Study #6 BEPS 11-05-01.) There is, however, no guidance here about what to do if your best efforts at persuasion fail, but for most students it seemed clear to them that they would not be a party to what they perceived as dishonesty (a cover-up) and the potential harm that could come to the organization, the buyers and their own career. They felt strongly that the buying public had a right to the information up front in order to make an informed buying decision. I was so proud.

But – a hand went up (actually, his hand didn't go up; students just speak up in these discussions). 'I disagree', said one student.

Everyone has a chance to take the floor in these discussions. I asked him to explain his position. As far as he was concerned, he said, since the contamination had been determined to be 'low-level' and 'not life-threatening' he felt no obligation whatsoever to broach this subject in the promotional materials. He was on the boss's side. He figured that there was no harm to be done, not disclosing the information was in no way misleading, and he was willing to make the decision for the potential buyers that they didn't need this information.

If other students in the class agreed with him, they weren't saying, and the response to this student was that his decision would be less than ethical. To this he responded that he guessed he would just have to make his own decision based on his own personal code of ethics.

USING PERSONAL VALUES

There is little doubt that personal values and selection of ethical principles to use for decision-making are just that – personal. In fact, I had contributed in no small way to his way of thinking because one of the early assignments that the students had to complete for this course was the development of a personal code of ethics and a document explaining their thought process in developing it.

This proved to be a very valuable exercise, according to the students. Almost to a person, they said that whereas they believed they had a fairly strong code of ethics to which they adhered, they had never actually thought about that code of behaviour in a systematic way. For example, they had never considered the specific values they held dear, nor their reasons for giving these values such high regard. The requirement to develop this code for a mark forced them into a very self-reflective mode.

So, for each of us, we have that personal code – whether or not we've ever taken the time to write it down – that guides our decision-making. Can it be relied upon?

Marshall Pittman and Robin Radtke, professors in the Department of Accounting at the University of Texas at San Antonio, conducted a study to determine whether employees use their personal code or the organizational ethics codes for decision-making.[5] The researchers found that most employees indicated that they have their own strong code of ethics and used that to guide their decisions. A good thing? Not really. When Pittman and Radtke asked these same employees ethical questions, many of them responded to the situations in a 'less than ethical fashion'.

What the results of this study said to me was that this student wasn't unlike many (perhaps most) people in the workplace today. Further, I realized that there was little I could do to change his mind. Personal ethical standards are deep-seated.

But does that make them 'right'? Is it good enough to have a personal code of ethics and to thumb your nose at what's conventionally expected of you as a professional?

This is where scholars of ethics have a problem with the notion of pluralism. If relativism, as we have discussed it previously, can be described as 'the view that moral principles or codes are relative to a society or even an individual',[6] then pluralism is an acceptance of the notion that there are different ethical approaches and in some people's view this means that each individual's ethical approach is valid. This is too simplistic for application to professional ethics situations, and very likely for personal ones. In fact, ethicists tend to think of pluralism as the notion that moral standards, norms or principles cannot be reduced to a single standard, norm or principle. That doesn't necessarily translate to the interpretation that my student gave to the situation: just because he has a different moral compass, that doesn't make his moral compass 'right' in the context of a profession that has some moral standards. However, unlike medical doctors, for example, we are not licensed professionals. Therefore, although a physician can be censured for failing to live up to acceptable ethical standards of practice, a public relations practitioner cannot. That does not imply, however, that there are no standards. It also doesn't suggest that being aware of your own personal code of ethics isn't an important first step in understanding your personal approach to making ethical decisions.

DEVELOPING YOUR OWN CODE

Notwithstanding the fact that your application of your personal code of ethics may not be as 'ethical' as you thought, giving some thought to creating one is a useful exercise that I highly recommend. Take a look at the questions in Figure 8.1. Consider each as carefully and thoughtfully as you can.

Try being brutally honest with yourself, and once you have the answers to these questions, try constructing a code of ethics that guides your own personal decision-making. Type it out neatly and have it laminated. Hang it on a wall in your office and look at it every time you're faced with a dilemma. It just might make you think twice, and really that's all we can hope for, isn't it?

Questions for creating your personal code

1. What kind of values did your parents try to instil into you as a child? Your church? School? Individual teachers? Mentors?

2. Which ones stuck with you?

3. What experiences in your childhood altered the way you value things in your life?

4. What experiences as an adult (both personal and professional) have had an impact on what you value?

5. To whom are you loyal? (Consider yourself, your employer/clients, your family, your profession, society for starters.)

6. What kind of ethical style do you have? (Try: virtuous, intuitive, empathetic, Darwinian or Machiavellian for starters, ie what principles appeal to you most?)

7. What have you done in your past when faced with ethical dilemmas?

Figure 8.1 *Questions for creating your personal code*

Notes

1. Center for the Study of Ethics in the Professions (Illinois Institute of Technology) [accessed 25 November 2003] *Codes of Ethics On-Line.* http://www.iit.edu/departments/csep/PublicWWW/codes/codes. html

2. International Association of Business Communicators [accessed 26 June 2001] *Code of Ethics for Professional Communicators.* http:// www.iabc.com/members/joining/code.htm

3. Global Alliance for Public Relations and Communication Management [accessed 25 November 2003] *Global Protocol on Ethics in Public Relations.* http://www.globalpr.org/knowledge/ethics/ consultation.asp

4. Public Relations Society of America Ethics Case Study Series. http://www.prsa.org
5. Pittman, Marshall and Radtke, Robin [accessed 26 June 2001] http://accounting.rutgers.edu/raw/aaa/2002annual/cpe/cpe3/tue 3.pdf
6. Wolf, S (1992) Two levels of pluralism, *Ethics*, **102** (4), p 786

9

Sex and the single (or not) PR practitioner: conflict of interest

To know what is right and not to do it is the worst cowardice.

Confucius

'Didn't I see you having dinner the other night with John Smith?'

It seems like an innocent enough question coming from a friend and colleague.

'Yes, we've been seeing each other for a while.'

Your friend looks at you, puzzled. ' Doesn't your PR firm represent one of his company's competitors?'

'Sure, but our relationship outside the office is strictly personal. What are you getting at?' You're beginning to become irritated at the direction of the conversation.

'Nothing, really,' your friend continues. ' You just might want to be careful. There are people who might not think it's such a good idea. Like your boss, for one.'

'Well,' you retort defensively, 'my personal life is my own business.'

And with that you sweep another potential ethical dilemma under the rug. Sex – or other personal relationships – and the public relations practitioner: can it be a conflict of interest or any other kind of moral dilemma?

DEFINING A CONFLICT

Simply put, a conflict of interest is a situation where one's personal interests conflict with one's professional ones. Dr Michael McDonald, Director of the University of British Columbia Centre for Applied Ethics, defines a conflict of interest as 'a situation in which a person, such as a public official, an employee, or a professional, has a private or personal interest sufficient to appear to influence the objective exercise of his or her duties'.[1] As you might have noticed from this definition, there is no need for the objective exercise of a person's work-related duties to be truly compromised, only that they 'appear' to be compromised.

Thus, using this definition, it seems clear that public relations professionals have a number of situations that present potential conflict situations, some of which are unique to PR, others that are common to all people in the work world today.

SLEEPING WITH... THE ENEMY?

Students often come up with the most interesting cases all by themselves. One year, in an assignment requiring senior public relations students to develop and test a strategy game based on public relations principles, one group developed an amazing prototype called 'PR Ethicmania'. One of the key requirements for the game was for players to solve ethical dilemmas. The proposed solution would then be judged by a consensus of opposing players in an attempt to arbitrate all those grey areas in ethics. One of the cases they presented went something like this:

> You have just landed your first public relations job after graduation. Your boss seems pleased with your work so far and invites you to attend an out-of-town seminar with him. You're delighted and infer that you are indeed doing well. Once away from the office together it becomes clear to you that his interest in you is less than professional; indeed, he's pressing for a more personal relationship, suggesting that you'll be very well rewarded within the organization. Do you (a) politely put him off and just go back to work forgetting about the whole thing; or (b) return to work and go to his boss with a sexual harassment complaint? (This case works whether you're a man or a woman, by the way.)

What seemed to me to be missing from this was yet another option: (c) go along with him and take the perks.

This whole case brought up a series of unanswered questions about the personal and professional relationships between public relations practitioners and their superiors, peers, clients, potential clients, competitors, media people, investors – the list seems to be endless.

In the case presented in the game situation, added on to the potential for a conflict of interest situation is the reality of a power imbalance.

This issue of carrying on a sexual relationship within what is otherwise a professional one is a dilemma that has plagued a number of other professions. The medical profession has been grappling with this one since Hippocrates said 'Whatever house I enter... I will stand free from any voluntary criminal action or corrupt deed and the seduction of females or males, be they slaves or free', in his famous Oath.

And while the issue seems to have been clearly defined for doctors – they are not permitted to carry on any kind of sexual relationship with current patients (although when a patient stops being current is hotly debated) and by definition it is considered to be sexual abuse – the issue is unclear for other professions, including PR. Relationships between public relations professionals and their clients or employers, for example, although different in some ways from that of a doctor and a patient, are nevertheless riddled with problems, both ethical and practical ones.

PRACTICALITIES BEFORE ETHICS

Apart from the murky ethical issues that these kinds of conflicting relationships raise, there are some very practical, everyday issues that bear consideration. Sometimes, dealing with the practical implications of a situation can help you to avoid the ethical ones altogether.

The first question that usually comes to mind is: what happens when the relationship is over? How will that affect the professional relationship between the protagonists or their relationships with their colleagues? Indeed, many organizations have ethical guidelines specifically prohibiting these liaisons to avoid the kinds of interpersonal and business problems that often arise.

Let's look first at the situation where you become involved with someone higher up on the organizational chart. The fundamental problem with this kind of relationship is like the physician's dilemma when dating a patient. The situation creates an imbalance of power and the potential for abuse. A person in a more powerful position can use that power to manipulate the other person in the relationship, whether consciously or unconsciously. And if the sexual advances are unwanted, this is at the very least considered to be harassment.

So, there is danger in the boss–underling relationship, mostly for the underling. What about the effects this relationship has on others? When the formal lines of communication within an organization are disrupted by these informal liaisons, suspicion can arise among the rest of the tribe. This suspicion can lead to distrust and can have an impact on the working relationships. When this happens, you are clearly facing a moral problem.

But what about personal relationships with your peers? And who among us has not been tempted to date someone at work? Indeed, isn't that where we often meet people? As silly as some organizations' rules against fraternization among employees might seem, and the ethical issues might be less clear, they have some real practical value. For many people, it's difficult, if not impossible, to make that clean break between personal and professional time when face-to-face with the beloved. It is difficult to get work done and this may, in fact, lead to the ethical problem of short-changing your employer who pays your salary.

Another practical question: how will this relationship be viewed by your colleagues? For people in the business of managing perceptions for our clients and employers, we are often less able to confront the issue of how our own behaviour will be perceived by those around us. When two people in a place of business have a personal relationship, it does affect the way their colleagues view them.

So it's clear that there are problems when you're sleeping with colleagues. That's not the only place where personal relationships can pose professional problems.

OUTSIDE CONFLICTS

Although the protagonist in our little scenario at the beginning of this chapter was not dating someone at her place of business, strictly speaking, in the field of public relations there are many people with whom a personal relationship can affect, or at the very least be perceived by others to be affecting, the professional one.

Are there any ethical implications in the establishment of personal liaisons with clients or potential clients? Perhaps we can learn something from the experience of the legal profession. Lawyers, too, face issues when confronted with a developing sexual relationship with a client. While lawyers cannot be disbarred for this behaviour – only cautioned – they are directed to terminate the professional relationship before continuing the personal one. This seems simple enough. A personal relationship changes the perceptions of the entire situation and can affect one's professional judgement. This is true of members of the legal profession and can certainly be true of PR professionals.

And then there is the situation of personal relationships with members of the media. Personal friendships, or more, with members of the media, one of our more important publics, have a number of ethical implications, both for the journalist and for the PR professional. Consider the following situation.

You are a female PR professional who begins dating a journalist you meet at the end of a press conference. You try to be discreet with your relationship, but sooner or later you are spotted and the rumours begin. 'Perhaps she's bribing him' is one perception. 'Perhaps she's leaking information to the media' is another possible perception of those who are observing. Either way, the situation, harmless as it may be, has the potential to be perceived as a bad situation – and a perception is really all that is necessary for the liaison to be labelled a conflict of interest.

The nature of PR's role within organizations, with its access to proprietary information, makes it very important to maintain a sense of decorum at all times – whether for the reality or the perception.

PERSONAL RELATIONSHIPS AND ETHICAL PRINCIPLES

It seems that there are several ethical principles worth consideration. First, there is a *confidentiality* issue. While it may be possible for a couple to carry on a personal relationship without ever once discussing business, in anything past a one-night stand it's hardly believable. Thus, there is the potential for proprietary information to leak from one source to an unplanned receiver. This might be information that a superior should keep from his or her underling, information that a competitor has no right to possess, or a story that a member of the media should not be privy to – all told under the umbrella of the bed sheet.

Second, there is a potential for professional *harm* to come to one or both members of the couple. Regardless of what they believe to be the 'strictly personal' nature of the relationship, how it is perceived by superiors, co-workers and clients, among others, will have the final say in the outcome professionally.

When it comes to assessing harm, it might be wise also to consider the potential harm to those around you. This begins with your immediate colleagues and spreads out from there. Is your relationship likely to be perceived as a problem by others outside the organization? In this way is it likely to have implications for your organization? As you begin to ask these questions, it becomes clear that a personal relationship between you and someone with whom you already have a professional relationship has much wider implications than simply for the two people involved.

Another principle that can be compromised is the issue of *truth*. To whom must you lie in an attempt to keep your relationship private? And, do you even have the right to privacy, given all of the other potential ethical conflicts?

Since there are no hard and fast guidelines for this kind of behaviour, it is wise to use some common sense and consider what is truly the right thing to do in these situations.

OTHER CONFLICT SITUATIONS

Personal relationships are certainly not the only situations within which a PR professional can find himself or herself in a potential conflict of interest situation, although they often seem to be the ones that tend to be glossed over as not truly important. Perhaps before we examine situations other than personal relationships that have the potential to present these problems, it might be useful to establish why we're even concerned about them. The short answer is this: trust.

Writing about conflicts of interest in government positions, political scientists Kenneth Kernaghan and John Langford make it clear: 'a primary reason for concern about conflicts of interest is that they reduce public trust and confidence'.[2] They could just as easily be writing about public relations professionals. As we have already established in an earlier chapter, trust between organizations and their publics, including society in general, is key to relationships that are the fundamental focus of public relations practice.

So, if trust is what is at stake, it is important to examine a few other situations outside personal relationships that also can present conflicts. Kernaghan and Langford have developed a list of potential conflict situations.[3] Let's use them as a basis for our list with examples applied specifically to PR.

1. *Self-dealing:* If a you are a PR practitioner working for an agency and award a sub-contract to a design firm that you personally own, this would be a self-dealing problem.
2. *Accepting benefits:* If you are an internal PR person, are involved in selecting a consulting agency to plan an event for your organization and one of the contenders provides you with dinner and free tickets to an event they are currently planning for someone else, this could be construed as accepting benefits. Influence peddling is another form of this practice.
3. *Using your employer's property for personal benefit:* If you are doing outside freelance work (not uncommon in PR) and decide to use the office photocopier to produce your materials to send to someone else

strictly for your own benefit, this is a conflict situation. This will come up again in our discussion of moonlighting in Chapter 10.

4. *Using confidential information:* This is one of the situations we were trying to avoid by limiting our personal relationships with clients, suppliers, the media and so on. It is possible to leak this confidential information inadvertently or deliberately. Either way, it's an ethical problem.

5. *Moonlighting:* Clearly, if your outside freelance work is for an organization that is a direct competitor to your employer or involves any of the other conflict situations that we've already discussed, then it is a problem.

6. *A past-employee:* Leaving a position and going to work for a competitor, for example, puts you in a potential conflict situation. You are privy to information that you do not have the right to use to benefit your new employer. And that might just be the reason you were hired!

So, what is one to do about these potential conflicts? There are really only two choices if you are attempting to be an ethical public relations practitioner. First, you can declare to all parties your potential conflicts and let them help you to decide if you can continue to behave in the same fashion. For example, you could tell your boss that you are doing freelance work and ask if it would be all right to use the photocopier. If he or she says yes (which I seriously doubt would be the case), then guidelines would be set up and you have avoided a conflict.

Indeed, one of the most recent contributions to dealing with the issue of employee dating is the implementation at some organizations of the so-called 'dating contract'. The relationship is openly declared to management and the parameters are set out with all parties signing. The document can cover guidelines for behaviour as well as the ramifications for the participants should the relationship begin to negatively affect their work or the work of others. The kind of full disclosure illustrated by this kind of solution to a potential problem is one of the ways of dealing with other situations where conflict of interest might otherwise be perceived.

Of course, the second choice is really the simplest: avoid any of these situations in the first place. To reflect on your potential for becoming involved in conflict-of-interest situations, consider the questions in Figure 9.1.

Avoiding conflicts of interest

Consider the following statements to reflect on your potential for falling into conflicts of interest.

☐   I keep my personal and professional relationships separate.
☐   I avoid discussing business in non-business situations.
☐   I disclose any outside business interests to my employer.
☐   I avoid accepting anything that could be viewed as a gift from potential clients.
☐   I avoid using any office equipment and supplies for tasks unrelated to my employer.
☐   I avoid taking care of personal business on company time.
☐   I feel comfortable in my ability to maintain employer/client confidentiality.

Figure 9.1   *Avoiding conflicts of interest*

Notes

1.   McDonald, Michael [accessed 2 October 2003] *Ethics and Conflict of Interest*. http://www.ethics.ubc.ca/mcdonald/conflict.html
2.   Kernaghan, Kenneth and Langford, John (1990) *The Responsible Public Servant*, Institute for Research on Public Policy, Halifax, NS, p 139
3.   Kernaghan and Langford, pp 142–53

10

You... against the world

A man may not always be what he appears to be, but what he appears to be is always a significant part of what he is.

Dr Willard Gaylin

As we have seen, there are ethical dilemmas inherent in your relationships at work and in your personal life, and you usually share these situations with others. There are, however, situations in which you must deal with a very personal issue and you must make your decision in relative isolation. These are personal crises of conscience. We'll examine two very personal ethical dilemmas that everyone in business, including public relations practitioners, can often face. These two specific situations are first, the issue of whistle-blowing and its less serious but equally confounding cousin, tattling; and second, the personal choice to moonlight.

A DILEMMA YOU DON'T NEED

It's Friday afternoon and you have almost completed preparations for a client pitch you have to make first thing on Monday morning. Your boss, the senior account manager, stops at your office door on his way out.

'Could you manage a new slide to add to the presentation?' he asks as he hands you a sheaf of papers. 'I have the new cost projections.'

You glance at them and notice that they are significantly different from the figures that had been discussed by the team earlier in the week.

'These don't look like the ones we discussed...'

'No,' he says, laughing. 'I massaged them a bit. The client will never know.' Although clearly pleased with himself, he seems to notice the frown that's growing on your face. 'It's just the way things are done', he says. 'I'll look forward to seeing those slides on Monday.' And he's gone.

You take a closer look and note that there seems to be more than a bit of a discrepancy and it occurs to you that this isn't the first time you've noticed your boss 'massaging things'. What should you do?

And if you think this is a difficult dilemma to find yourself in, what would you do if the situation were even larger? How would you deal with stumbling upon clear evidence that the organization you work for are engaged in activities that are potentially harmful to the health or welfare of the public? The situation is larger than you are, but the decision about your behaviour is deep within your own conscience.

These are questions of personal ethics that public relations professionals, along with everyone else in the working world today, can find themselves confronting from time to time. Your professional code of ethics won't help you out here.

A CONTINUUM OF TATTLING

If we look back at the history of modern public relations in the United States of the early 20th century, we often identify the era of muckraking journalism as the beginning of the need for organizations to consider hiring public relations counsellors. The so-called muckrakers took upon themselves the job of exposing the truth of offensive and dangerous behaviour of organizations at the time. They took pride in accomplishing what the employees had been unable to do. This was lauded as a very highly moral act. However, telling tales when you are actually working for the organization in question is not necessarily praised by business today. So, public relations has a long history of association with the notion of telling tales in business – albeit often from the other side!

What we are really dealing with is a continuum of disclosure that runs from simple tattling, for lack of a better word, to whistle-blowing. You observe a colleague slipping pens, pencils and computer paper into her briefcase while the rest of the department is trying to figure out how supplies keep disappearing. You overhear a colleague telling someone that she falsified some budget figures. These situations are ones that put you in a position of deciding whether or not to 'tell on' your colleague. Technically, you're not really whistle-blowing as the term is currently defined in business.

Although the definitions vary, whistle-blowing is generally defined as disclosing publicly unethical conduct observed in the workplace – conduct that could result in harm to the public. This unethical behaviour runs the gamut from environmental hazards, to health risks, to theft, to corruption. In these days of what appears to amount to institutionalized corruption, it seems an even more salient topic for discussion than ever. These are serious ethical breaches – something more than reporting colleagues for their creative approaches to stocking their home offices. What's more, the person doing the whistling is often still working for the organization in question.

HOW TO BE A WHISTLE-BLOWER

How do you know when to take action and come forward to disclose such information? There seems little doubt that it is a particularly scary prospect with ramifications that may be beyond even what the potential whistle-blower is able to imagine. But knowing that you should do it is really one of those matters of personal conscience. If you know harm is being done and you have the power to stop it, the ethical course of action seems clear. Actually doing it, however, is not so simple.

Your first step involves only you. At this stage you may not have actual proof that what you think is going on is truly the case. However, if you have any evidence of wrongdoing on the part of the organization you work for, you have a dilemma on your hands. First, you need to consider the extent of the harm or potential harm that is being caused. These are steps that you alone generally take. If you determine that harm is being done, your next step would be to try to deal with the situation internally. Go to your superiors. Determine their reactions. See if they will take the action that needs to be taken to mitigate any harm. Once you have exhausted all internal channels and nothing has changed, then, before going public (which actually makes you a whistle-blower by definition – up until now you're just a concerned employee), you need to ensure that you have concrete evidence to back up your allegations. Finally, you need to consider whether going public is actually likely to have any impact on the situation. But make no mistake, going public to blow the whistle on unethical behaviour you observe in your workplace can and does have consequences – largely for you.

Weighing the consequences

One newspaper columnist writing about whistle-blowing suggests, not so subtly, that more people would report things 'if they felt protected from retaliation'.[1] This issue of retaliation is one of the most serious considerations for those who otherwise consider it critical to blow the whistle.

In the United Kingdom, whistle-blowers are protected under the Public Interest Disclosure Act of 1998. It defines 'protected disclosures' as ones where (a) criminal activity is being or is likely to be carried out, (b) there is a real or likely miscarriage of justice, (c) health or safety is being or likely to be endangered, or (d) the environment is currently being damaged or is likely to be.[2]

In the United States there is also legislation to protect people who come forward (making a distinction between bona fide whistle-blowing and personal complaints), but that is not the case in all countries. For example, Canadians are not so lucky. At the time of writing, according to Melanson,[3] there is only one Canadian province with such laws.

But even if there is legislation to protect you from harassment and overt retaliation, there is the more subtle kind of recrimination that might come the way of whistle-blowers. Whereas it might seem that a person who would report such activities holds high moral standards and would be an employee to be coveted, business today does not necessarily see it that way. A reputation as a whistle-blower is not lauded in all circles. Thus whistle-blowers do so at their peril, based on a personal value system that will guide them to do what they believe is right. There is a certain comfort in staying true to yourself and your own values.

TATTLING

Where does that leave those situations where there is no real harm to the public perceived, but there is clearly a breach of ethical behaviour (petty theft, massaging budgets to deceive potential clients, etc)? Obviously, you need to consider the consequences for you personally, but in the end, again, you have to be true to your own values, ensuring that what you are doing is not motivated by petty issues such as professional jealousy or personal dislike of an individual.

If your workplace has no formal mechanism for anonymous reporting of such behaviour (which in itself can be a problem if there is overt encouragement of people to rat on one another), your best first step would be to confront the individual. This is akin to trying to deal with a potential whistle-blowing situation internally before going outside. If this has no effect (sometimes the perpetrator will change his or her behaviour when confronted), then you need to consider going to a higher authority, but only if you have solid evidence to support your allegations and if you have decided that it's worth it.

In the end it's a true personal decision. Just answer the question: Can I live with myself if I do it? Can I live with myself if I don't?

THE TEMPTATIONS OF MOONLIGHTING

'How'd you like to make some extra money?' says the voice on the other end of the telephone.

What immediately springs to mind? Oh no, another multi-level marketing scheme? Or, like many (most?) people in the public relations business who receive calls like this from time to time, do you recognize when someone wants you to use your skills to do paid work outside of your regular job? In other words, how do you respond to offers to moon-light?

One of the great advantages of the field of public relations is the kind of flexibility that's afforded in the job market. This translates into many opportunities to find your own little niche and be an entrepreneur if you choose, or to do extra work when someone needs your expertise. And I hardly know a PR practitioner, myself included, who hasn't dabbled in outside work from time to time. This is another of those true personal decisions, but what, if any, are the ethical issues involved?

Why moonlight?

The reasons people in public relations moonlight are as individual as the people doing it. Some of the most common include taking advantage of opportunities to enhance a portfolio or to gain experience in areas that might not be part of the 'day job'. In addition, those who are considering self-employment often use this approach to ease into that self-employ-ment without loss of a regular pay cheque. Others do it because they don't really like their regular job and are exploring other areas and making new contacts before taking the final step of moving on. Perhaps the most common reason is to make extra money. And while there is nothing inherently wrong in making extra money or gaining more experience, there are some moral boundaries over which an ethical practitioner dare not step.

The ethical quagmire

The big question here is not if you *can* moonlight (there are plenty of opportunities for those who seek them), but rather *should* you?

Just as with all other ethical questions, there is no black and white answer. It's not a simple matter of yes you should, or no you should not. It's more a matter of examining the ethical problems and looking at the varying situations, some of which pose more of an ethical problem than others.

Here are some of the potential pitfalls:

- *Conflict of interest:* Will the work for, or representation of, a particular client in any way put you in a conflict of interest situation with your current employer? If this potential client is a competitor, for example, you will have access to information on both sides that is not yours to share. Indeed, even if you vow never to use such information, remember what we always say about journalists – there's no such thing as 'off the record'. Even the appearance that you may be in a conflict situation is enough to make this a morally unacceptable choice. You might want to review our discussion of conflicts in Chapter 9.

- *Truth telling:* Do you feel that you'd have to hide what you are doing from your employer or colleagues at your regular job? By hiding your activities you may be deceiving by omission at the very least. If your response to this is that you are entitled to do what you want on your off hours, consider why you are so vehement about this. Your motivation may be the real key to your discomfort with openness.

- *Stealing:* Yes, stealing. This can take many forms. Will you be doing any of this work on your employer's time? Will you be using any materials or equipment at your office (computer, software, postage, paper, photocopier)? This all constitutes stealing and is unacceptable for an ethical practitioner. If you are using your employer's time or resources for private gain, you are not behaving professionally or ethically.

- *Harm to others:* Is there any possibility that anyone will be harmed if you do this? This is a tough one for many. Who could possibly be harmed? Your daylight employer, clients and colleagues spring immediately to mind if your off-duty work causes you to be less sharp and focused on the job. You can only spread yourself so thin. In addition, are you violating any part of your contractual arrangements with your employer – have you agreed not to do certain kinds of outside work?

Perhaps one of the most important steps you can take to avoid any possibility of falling into ethically treacherous territory and still fulfil your desire to moonlight would be to ensure that your employer is clear about the kind of work you are doing outside work hours, and is agreeable to this.

Codes can help

The codes of conduct produced by most professional public relations associations can provide us with a bit of guidance. The code of the Canadian Public Relations Society[4] is especially helpful in setting up ethical parameters for such outside work:

- One useful tenet of the code says 'A member shall deal fairly with past or present employers/clients, fellow practitioners and members of other professions.' You deal fairly with your employer by ensuring that your outside work does not interfere with the work you have contracted to do during the daylight hours.
- Another principle says 'Members shall be prepared to disclose the names of their employers or clients for whom public communications are made and refrain from associating themselves with anyone who would not respect such policy.' Being able to disclose the names of your outside clients keeps the work and your reputation transparent and above reproach.
- The code also says 'A member shall protect the confidences of present, former and prospective employers/clients' and...
- 'A member shall not represent conflicting or competing interests without the expressed consent of those concerned, given after a full disclosure of the facts.'

Personal ethical decisions are just that – personal. Sometimes it seems like it's just you against the world, but often if we look outside ourselves, we see that there are others who have faced similar decisions and have lived to tell the tale and to prosper.

Notes

1. Melanson, Rosella [accessed 23 October 2002] Whistleblowing: breaking the silence of the lambs (column first published in the *New Brunswick Telegraph Journal*, May 2001). http://personal.nbnet. nb.ca/rosellam/whistleblowing.html
2. Government of the United Kingdom [accessed 10 July 2003] Public Interest Disclosure Act of 1998. http://www.hmso.gov.uk/ acts/acts1998/80023–a.htm#1
3. Melanson, R
4. Canadian Public Relations Society [accessed 10 July 2003] Code of Ethics. http://www.cprs.ca/english/membership/e_mem bership_code.htm

Part 3

Strategies and dilemmas

Now that we have examined what kinds of principles and values lie beneath ethical decision-making and looked at some personal ethical predicaments that can befall public relations practitioners, we need to apply this to some actual day-to-day aspects of our practice.

Public relations in the 21st century is a strategic management function that uses communication strategies to help to build and maintain relationships between organizations and their publics. In practice, that includes everything from developing the most complex promotional plans to the more mundane aspects of everyday dealings with the media and even putting together the employee website or print newsletter, and everything in between. Although we often move from one function within our diverse positions to another without a thought about the ethics of what we are doing, even simple decisions and actions can have a moral component. Let's face it, much of what we do is what is termed amoral – having no moral implications at all. Consider choosing the colour for your new company logo – hardly an ethical issue unless choice of a colour has certain unethical implications for specific publics. Hard to get away from it, isn't it?

Part 3 will provide you with an opportunity to think more deeply about aspects of your job whose ethical implications you may have overlooked. Everything from choosing clients to the relationship between simple bad taste and ethics are some of the topics that are frequently overlooked by PR practitioners aiming for a more ethical practice.

11

PR ethics and the media: the old and the new

The pure and simple truth is rarely pure and never simple.
                                Oscar Wilde (*The Importance of Being Earnest*)

There is no other aspect of public communication that is as closely associated with public relations as is the media. We undertake all manner of day-to-day technical activities in relation to the media: we send media releases, create media kits and conduct media conferences, pitch stories to cynical journalists, subject ourselves to interviews, prepare others in our organization for media interviews – the list goes on. Add onto that the more strategic functions associated with developing long-term plans for nurturing media relationships and using mass media channels to communicate messages, and it is understandable why so many people outside our field seem to think that media relations is synonymous with public relations. Some seem to believe that it's all we do: certainly journalists often do. We know better; it is but one part of what we do, but it is a very important one and perhaps the most high-profile. For that reason, considerations of the ethics of how we strategize about and deal on a day-to-day basis with media are very important. In addition, when it comes to a modern discussion of ethics in the media we need to consider not only traditional media (print, television, radio) but also the so-called 'new media'. This new media encompasses the new social media or, as some have dubbed it, 'Web 2.0'. If we thought that our relationship with the traditional media was fraught with ethical landmines, the ethical issues inherent in the current and future applications of social media to public relations programming are just beginning to emerge. We'll examine a number of ethical issues in both traditional media and social media.

OUR RELATIONSHIP WITH JOURNALISTS

The truth is that journalists need public relations people every bit as much as PR people need journalists. In fact, even the journalism literature suggests that some 40–50 per cent or more of all the news that's reported on any given day originated in PR departments in business, government and non-profit organizations. This means that the relationship between public relations practitioners and journalists is very significant; there are, however, ethical dilemmas inherent in the very nature of the relationship.

The character of the relationship between public relations and the media is often at the heart of the potential ethical conflicts. While we're all clear that many, perhaps most, journalists consider us to be, at the very least, manipulators of the truth, perhaps we could consider what Janet Malcolm wrote in the 13 March 1989 issue of *The New Yorker:* 'Every journalist who is not too stupid or too full of himself to notice what is going on knows that what he does is morally indefensible. He is a kind of confidence man, preying on people's vanity, ignorance, or loneliness, gaining their trust and betraying them without remorse.'

So it seems that the two fields are on a pretty even footing when it comes to the moral high ground (or low ground). What, then, are the issues that can get in the way of an ethical relationship?

The two big issues that emerge are honesty in our communication and access – access *to* media and access *by* media. Both of these potentially problematic issues can affect not only the relationship between public relations and the media, but also between organizations and their communities that use the media as a conduit for information.

Every single public relations textbook on the market today touts honesty as the cornerstone for your media relations policies. That fact would probably come as quite a revelation for most journalists I know. Indeed, the moniker 'spin doctors', which is applied by almost everyone to public relations flacks (there's another one that has rather unpleasant implications about the ethics of those who fill those positions – us), in itself tells a story about a less-than-honourable approach to communicating with the media and consequently with a wider public. The truth is that the name is not so far from the truth. Before you start protesting your own honesty, we need to consider that most of the dishonest things about public relations are much more subtle than the outright lie. They are so insidious that we often overlook them.

Several years ago, a PR agency in my home town issued faxes to local media outlets indicating that there 'will likely' be a major news conference at 9:30 am the following day at a 'location to be determined'. The final teaser was to suggest that later on that day they would have further information available. It seemed an odd PR strategy even if it didn't smack of an ethical breach. There will 'likely' be a news conference? Whoever heard of sending out a news release suggesting there 'might' be a news conference, which of course also suggests that there just as easily 'might not'?

It seemed clear that this was some kind of a ploy, a public relations stunt if you like. The release, however, was reported on in the local media, not as the issuers might have hoped, but rather under a headline that read 'Mysterious fax sparks media's mistrust', thereby allowing the reporter to write not about whatever event the PR agency might have wanted to publicize, but about how devious PR people can be. By failing to provide details, and thus keeping the media on a string, the media were quite correct in their conclusion that this was somehow oblique and thereby perceived as shifty. This kind of PR strategy is just the kind of approach that alienates the media and plays havoc with the relationship. The development of mistrust between PR people and the media is problematic. But why is it an ethical issue?

Journalist and media trainer Ed Shiller put it this way: 'When the media and their primary sources of information become estranged, only the truth will suffer.'[1] It is this issue of mangling the truth of the communication that eventually reaches the public that is at the heart of the ethical problem. Clearly, when the public is not receiving honest, truthful information, then they are being wronged – harmed. When the mistrust that often seems inherent in the relationship between PR and the media (or at least between individual reporters and individual PR practitioners) affects the process of honest public communication, then it is a moral issue.

MEDIA ACCESS AND ETHICS

The second issue, which includes media access as well as access to the media, provides us with just as much to consider as the issue of honesty or lack thereof.

It seems clear to most of us who have experience in dealing with the media that the media believe that they have a certain inalienable right to access to information and sources. Often, however, the needs of organizations and individuals within those organizations conflict with those so-called rights. Running into a brick wall can initiate a host of media behaviours that run the gamut from simple rudeness to more aggressive attempts to secure the information. These kinds of behaviours on the part of reporters contribute to the mistrust in the relationship between PR and the media.

Perhaps even more problematic from our point of view in trying to practise our profession ethically is the question of gaining access to the media. Whereas we all recognize that bribing the media to cover a story is not only unwise but completely unethical, where do you draw the line?

Consider the following case. A former, local university president was well known for many seasons for his annual media Christmas parties. For years he threw open the doors to the presidential mansion and fêted the local media – no special treatment for any specific reporters or outlets, mind you. Rather than limiting it to those reporters who had provided positive coverage of the university's activities over the year, everyone was invited to the open house. Indeed, even reporters who would blanch at the thought of taking an incentive from a source looked forward to the event.

Was this a terrifically creative public relations strategy (one which was not attempted by any of the other local universities), or a questionable ethical practice? Was this a case of subtle bribery, or an honest attempt to develop a stronger relationship between an organization and one of its important publics? Whereas there are no specific guidelines about what size a 'gift' must be to constitute bribery, or even if an invitation to a party qualifies as a 'gift', there is always a need not only to behave in an ethical way, but also to be perceived to be doing so. The first step, however, is simply to be aware that there is a potential moral issue here. And that is one more step than most PR professionals might take in this situation.

JOURNALISTS HAVE CODES, TOO

Most journalists seem to enter their chosen field because of a true desire to uncover and report to the public on the truth. As we examine the media today, however, it seems that sensationalism, inaccuracies and superficiality are rampant. There is little doubt about from where the current scepticism of the public about the press arises. Journalists, however, like public relations practitioners, have codes of ethics. A quick examination of what their codes tell them may just lead us to the conclusion that we're not all so different – that just maybe we are indeed all singing the same song, just in different keys.

A quick visit to EthicNet,[2] an online database of European Codes of Journalism Ethics which provides the codes from 36 countries from Armenia to the United Kingdom, suggests that what various professional associations of journalists believe is acceptable ethical behaviour is strikingly similar from one country to another.

The codes tout honesty and accuracy in all collection and dissemination of information, protection of confidentiality when necessary, fairness, and avoidance of bribes (ie anything for private advantage). What journalists are trying to accomplish in terms of public communication is no different from what we, as PR professionals, strive for. If, in fact, we're not so different after all, perhaps it is simply time that we worked on improving the relationship so that we can all work together for the good of society.

ASPECTS OF ETHICAL MEDIA RELATIONS

If media relations is a part of public relations that is not likely to change any time soon, it seems that it might be in our best interests and those of our publics if we take action to improve the ethics of our media relationships.

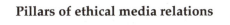

Pillars of ethical media relations

Honesty and accuracy
Judiciousness
Responsiveness
Respect

Clearly, above all, it is in the best interest of the community and our relationship with the media to adopt a policy of *honesty and accuracy* in all our dealings with the media. This does not necessarily mean full disclosure, but it does mean that when a decision is made to withhold information, this does not result in anyone being misled. Information that is misleading is just as dishonest as information that is an outright lie.

Being *judicious* about when and how you use the media means that a PR professional avoids clogging the channels of public communication with non-news and even pseudo-news. This has harmful effects on the public as well as on the element of trust in the relationship between PR and the media.

Responsiveness to the media is one of the most important lubricants of the trust in the relationship. Taking media calls and returning media calls may seem like just a good, strategic approach to building the relationship, but it has enormous impact on that all-important trust.

Finally, acting in a professional and *respectful* manner at all times, even in the face of rudeness or worse, is a fundamental aspect of an ethical relationship – whether with the media or with anyone else. Treating others respectfully is the first step to highly moral interactions. Perhaps now would be a good time to review Chapter 7, where we more fully discussed the fundamental ethical concept of respect.

The bottom line is that a lack of trust in the relationship between the public relations profession and the media is fundamentally an ethical conundrum. Actions that contribute to the mistrust are always ethically questionable. Ethics, then, seems to have a seriously important strategic aspect and perhaps it has an even larger and potentially more important role to play in society. The question we need to explore now is: What is PR's role in maintaining media transparency?

MEDIA TRANSPARENCY AND PR ETHICS

What does it mean for the media to be 'transparent'? If something is transparent, we generally think of being able to 'see through' it. Thus if something is transparent, then what lies beneath it can be seen. In large part, when searching for what lies beneath the media, we follow the money. This money trail involves issues of ownership, influence and control. It also includes responsible reporting that provides media consumers with enough information to make their own decisions about the legitimacy of the information presented to them, whether it originated with public relations or was ferreted out by journalists themselves.

For example, have you ever wondered about the extent to which a travel magazine's articles might be influenced by subsidization from the travel industry? Would your perception of the objectivity of a travel reporter's evaluation of a resort, for instance, be changed if you knew that he or she had been given an all-expenses-paid trip to that resort? Would you think differently of the resort's public relations staff if they were the ones who arranged this payment? Is this a bribe? Does it make it less of a bribe if this subsidization is disclosed? These are the kinds of questions that are relevant to the ethics of media transparency and public relations' role, which is intertwined with that of the media outlets themselves.

In 2001, the International Public Relations Association (IPRA) launched a media transparency campaign with a research study to determine the magnitude of the problem. With 242 member respondents representing 54 countries, they began to see a picture emerge.

For example, when asked if publications refuse to accept free travel, accommodation or products, 50 per cent of the North American respondents indicated that they *never refuse*. An overwhelming 87 per cent in Eastern Europe and 85 per cent in Southern Europe said they *never refuse* such offers. Twenty per cent of the North American respondents said that they believe print advertisements are *often* produced to look like editorial content with no indication to the reader that they are advertisements, and the percentage who believe this happens often is even larger in other parts of the world. I was, however, gratified to see that not one respondent from Canada or the United States believed that journalists there often take payments for the publication of specific news releases. (The report I read didn't, however, indicate complete results, so I don't know how many thought it happened at all). I was, however, perhaps naively shocked to see that the Canadians responding to the survey did say that exchange of money for coverage happens sometimes.[3]

So, it appears that there is indeed a problem with media transparency, and the public relations industry seems to be in bed with the media in many of these instances.

Melvin Sharpe, an American PR professor, was quoted by IPRA as saying 'Public relations has a vital check and balance relationship with journalism. It is our responsibility as a profession to keep the media ethical, transparent, responsible and accurate just as the media... has [sic] a public responsibility to inform and question and analyse the behaviours of the organisations and governments we advise.'[4] This sentiment captures the essence of what we need to do. Here are some practical approaches to doing your part to safeguard media transparency:

- Ensure that your advertising clearly indicates that it is such and not designed in such a way as to mislead the public into thinking that it is news copy.
- Indicate to reporters that you expect that the fact that they sampled your product or slept in your hotel for free will be clearly indicated in the piece.
- Never offer a journalist anything in exchange for favourable reporting.
- Never offer a journalist an enticement for killing a negative story.
- Never suggest that video news release (VNR) footage should be used without its clear identification that it is in fact a VNR.

A bonus to this approach to playing your part in maintaining media transparency is that in the long term it will actually enhance your relationship with journalists, which can only have strategic advantages. However, what about those new situations where your use of the media is, in fact, not mediated by journalists? This is the new ethical challenge of social media.

PR ETHICS AND THE NEW SOCIAL ORDER

The new social media have been referred to as a case of letting the inmates take over the asylum, to paraphrase a line from *One Flew Over the Cuckoo's Nest*. User-generated online communities and materials have added a new and only sometimes welcome addition to the communication arsenal of pubic relations and corporate communication. And as actor Charlie Chaplin is quoted as famously saying, 'Man is an animal with primary instincts of survival. Consequently, his ingenuity has developed first and his soul afterward. Thus the progress of science is far ahead of man's ethical behaviour.' The technological advances that are clearly illustrated by applications of social software have taken hold long before business and society as a whole considered the moral consequences of the activities.

In the fall of 2006, a blog[5] called 'Wal-Mart Across America' went live. Authored by a down-home, middle-America couple named Jim and Laura, it chronicled their journey across America in a recreational vehicle (RV), spending their overnights in Wal-Mart parking lots and visiting Wal-Mart stores along the way.[6] Their posts to their blog were full of praise for the wonders of Wal-Mart staff and stores. Since Wal-Mart had long held a reputation as a stingy employer, among other things, suspicions soon arose as to the veracity of the posts, and even to the identity of the couple ostensibly writing the blog. One person who became particularly curious was a professor at Colorado State University named Jonathan Rees, a labour historian, who wrote an open letter to them demanding that they reveal themselves.[7]

Professor Rees was truly on to something, and just what a can of worms he would open, public relations practitioners around the world should have been able to predict. It came to light that Jim and Laura, two real people (one a photographer and one a writer), were subsidized by the public relations firm Edelman, on behalf of their client Wal-Mart, as part of a strategy to counter criticism from union-supported groups that had formed to protest against Wal-Mart's labour policies.

While there are few rules about ethics and etiquette in the blogosphere, one unwritten rule had been broken: bloggers and all who read those blogs evidently expect truthfulness in identification of the writers. The fact that these bloggers were paid by Wal-Mart was not revealed and materially changed the perceptions of their blog posts – indeed, it could be said that it changed the truth of them. Edelman has since taken steps to enhance its ethical processes in dealing with the new technologies.[8]

Blogging as part of a larger public relations strategy is fast becoming an important component. Blogs have been used for developing internal relationships, developing and maintaining community relationships and involvement, engaging important publics in dialogue and providing information, to give just a few examples. Indeed, more and more PR professionals are being faced with clients and employers who will request, and sometimes demand, that the professional communicators take over these blogs. As can been seen by the Wal-Mart/Edelman debacle, this is not without its ethical considerations. And blogs are but one of the new technologies that present potentially explosive ethical dilemmas.

Also in 2006, a video clip spoof of the environmental documentary *An Inconvenient Truth* was posted on the video-sharing site YouTube. YouTube was originally developed as a place where amateur video buffs could post the results of their work and have others comment on them, but has morphed into something far more, including both amateur and professionally produced videos with a variety of objectives. The video in question was purportedly produced as an amateur piece by a 29-year-old Californian. Journalists at the *Wall Street Journal*, however, discovered that the producer of this video was in fact a lobbying firm whose clients included a large petroleum producer. Two American public relations scholars decided to determine whether, apart from the obvious transgressions of accepted ethical standards regarding disclosure of sponsorship, this kind of covert activity would have an impact on the intended PR effects of such a communication tool.[9] Although the results of their study did not support their hypothesis that inoculating the viewers against the message of such a video would change their perception, they did find a 'backlash effect on the producer of the ethically suspicious video'.[10] This kind of backlash against the sender of a message after ethical transgressions are discovered is not uncommon and, although it provides compelling arguments to us in the field of public relations to maintain ethical standards, the motivation for subsequent ethical decisions is morally suspect. What, then, can we do to deal with these emerging technologies?

This user-generated social media is probably here to stay and the temptations of plunging in head first are very tempting. These can be very effective tools for reputation management and relationship building, the cornerstones of public relations strategy. However, ethics needs to be a part of that strategic decision-making.

The Canadian Public Relations Society has published a policy statement on *Communications in Social Media*.[11] In it the authors refer back to the relevant tenets of the CPRS Code of Professional Standards, with specific reference to statements that refer to honesty, accuracy, integrity and truth. The UK's Chartered Institute of Public Relations (CIPR) has also weighed in on the subject. The CIPR *Social Media Guidelines* highlight making the public interest a priority, authorship and transparency, and professional competence. In addition, the CIPR focuses on the need to maintain confidentiality of privileged information when using social media.[12]

Media, whether traditional or the new so-called Web 2.0 type, are powerful tools for conveying messages and nurturing reputations and relationships. Just as with any tool or tactic, however, the overall strategy under which it is employed needs to consider the ethical implications. We might do well to consider the Word of Mouth Marketing Association's abbreviated Code of Conduct. Although they focus on the new media, the three tenets are important in all media communication. Their ROI rules are as follows:

*Honesty of **relationship:** you say who you're speaking for.*
*Honesty of **opinion:** you say what you believe.*
*Honesty of **identity:** you never obscure your identity.*[13]

Notes

1. Shiller, E (1994) *The Canadian Guide to Managing the Media*, Prentice Hall Canada Ltd, Scarborough, Ontario, p 13
2. EthicNet [accessed 9 October 2003] European Codes of Journalism Ethics. http://www.uta.fi/ethicnet/
3. More information on this study and IPRA's concerns about media transparency can be accessed at http://www.ipra.org/campaigns/campaigns.htm
4. Quoted in IPRA study.
5. I am assuming the reader has some familiarity with the terminology of social media.
6. According to 2007 Global Fortune 500 statistics, Wal-Mart is the largest public corporation in the world, by revenue.
7. Gogoi, Pallavi (2006) Wal-mart's Jim and Laura: the real story, *Business Week*, 8 October
8. For more information on Edelman's concerns, listen to their podcast Ethics in Social Media Communications, http://www.edelman.com/podcasts/ShowOnePodcast.asp?ID=125
9. Lim, J and Ki, E (2006) Resistance to ethically suspicious video spoof on YouTube: a test of inoculation theory, *Proceedings of the 10th International Institute for Public Relations Research*, pp 283–297
10. Lim and Ki, Ibid, p 283
11. Canadian Public Relations Society [accessed 28 November 2007] Policy statement: communications in social media, http://www.cprs.ca/files/CPRSPolicy-SocialMedia.pdf
12. Chartered Institute of Public Relations [accessed 28 November 2007] Social media and the CIPR Code of Conduct, http://www.cipr.co.uk/socialmedia/
13. Word of Mouth Marketing Association [accessed 28 November 2007] Code of Ethics, http://www.womma.org/ethics/code/

12

Persuasion... or propaganda?

Truthful words are not beautiful; beautiful words are not truthful. Good words are not persuasive; persuasive words are not good.

Lao-Tzu

Public relations practitioners today have a variety of roles, from the purely technical to the respected counsellor within organizations of every kind, from huge profit-making conglomerates to small grassroots not-for-profits and everything in between. Regardless of the role, however, PR people and the managerial function they represent must take on the position of advocate. It is simply the nature of what we do. Further, in advocating on behalf of an organization, person or cause, we often find ourselves in the position of having to persuade others to our point of view. How we go about doing that is what makes advocacy and persuasion bullseyes for ethical quagmires. In the name of strategic persuasion, public relations practitioners have, over the years, resorted to a variety of techniques that hover on the border between persuasion and blatant propaganda, or between the truth and lying by omission. We'll examine the ethical issues inherent in the persuasion process and then illustrate this with three discussions. First, we'll examine how the ethical role of PR advocate speaks to the need for careful selection of clients, employers and causes. Second, we'll focus on how the words we choose to convey our messages can have ethical consequences. Finally, we will examine that particular public relations strategy: the development and implementation of the so-called front group.

ENGINEERING CONSENT

You have an issue that your organization needs to increase public awareness about so that they understand it and change their behaviour to support the organizational point of view. Your approach is to devise a public relations strategy with just such objectives; you implement it and later determine that you were successful. This is the heart and soul of modern PR.

In 1947, however, Edward Bernays called it 'the engineering of consent'. And he believed that this apparent manipulation of ideas could – and indeed should – be carried out by the intellectual elite of society, of which, in his opinion, he was one. If you subscribe to the notion that Bernays can be called the father of modern public relations, as so many North American public relations practitioners do, then this is his legacy and the premise upon which modern public relations practice has evolved. It's little wonder that PR's advocacy role has been misunderstood and maligned for years, confused as it has been with the manipulation of the public mind.

In the field of public relations, an advocate is someone who speaks or acts in defence of an organization, issue or point of view – it is often our *raison d'être*. Regardless of whether you are speaking on behalf of a bank, a hospital, a government agency or a tobacco company, you are their advocate in the public's eye – you are inextricably identified with that organization or cause for everyone who sees or hears you or even knows what you do for a living. As we shall see with our illustration, it stands to reason that you would not represent a cause in which you do not believe: it wouldn't be ethical. If you are a staunch non-smoker, for example, working in public relations for a tobacco company puts you in a distinct conflict of interest situation. And the situation only gets worse when you have to extend that role of speaking in defence of your employer or client to having to plan to persuade others to that point of view. To speak in favour of a cause or issue that you actually oppose is nothing short of lying.

Advocacy, by its very nature, almost always leads to the need for persuasion. And, in the eyes of many, persuasion equals propaganda and manipulation. That's because in PR we are spin doctors, manipulators, experts in hyperbole and exaggeration, purveyors of PR ploys and organized lying – and that's just what they say about us every day in the newspapers.

ETHICAL PERSUASION... AN OXYMORON?

If you consider yourself to be a public relations person of integrity, how then can you ensure that your strategies designed to influence the public's attitudes and opinions (persuade) to your point of view – which by the way is a perfectly acceptable approach in a democratic society – are ethical and above reproach?

First, you need to understand the difference between persuasion and propaganda. While both are attempts to alter people's opinions and attitudes, propagandists do so only to satisfy the needs of the propagandist. In contrast, persuasion takes into consideration the mutual benefit of both the persuader and those being persuaded. Sounds like socially responsible communication, doesn't it?

Second, there are some very practical considerations for you as the purveyor of the persuasive messages if you want to ensure that you maintain a high degree of integrity in what you're doing.

There are some concrete steps that we can take to avoid the label of propaganda in persuasive communication. Here are some of those:

- Avoid false, fabricated, misrepresented, distorted or irrelevant evidence to support your point of view.
- Avoid intentionally specious, unsupported or illogical reasoning.
- Avoid trying to divert the public's attention by using such approaches as smear campaigns, or evoking intense emotions related to bigotry, God or the devil.
- Avoid asking your public to link your idea to emotion-laden values, motives or goals to which it is not really related.
- Don't conceal your real purpose (or the real supporters of your cause).
- Don't oversimplify complex situations into simplistic, two-valued either/or polar views or choices.[1]

And finally, the one that I think we all need to consider seriously:

- Avoid taking on the role of advocate for something in which you yourself do not believe.

Examine the projects and campaigns you have been involved in lately. Are you guilty of manipulation and propaganda? Even if you fail to recognize it, when it's there you can be certain that someone else will – and they'll call you on it.

PR FOR BIKER GANGS?

There's an old saying in ethics circles: just because you *can* do something, doesn't mean you *should* do it. Being able to do something is simply a matter of acquiring and using the necessary expertise; knowing when you should do something relies on your own ability to make ethical decisions.

So, you think you can 'do PR' for a biker gang? For a military dictatorship? For a crime boss? For a tobacco company? I have no doubt that a well-qualified public relations practitioner would be entirely capable of applying those qualifications to the PR problems and opportunities of just about any client. If you haven't yet seen the movie *Thank You for Smoking* now would be a good time. The question is: is it ethical? And one other thing: what does selecting a questionable client do for your professional reputation?

ANY CLIENT, ANY TIME?

Public relations columnist Jim Dingwall wrote an interesting article some years ago in the online publication *PR Canada* that provides us chapter and verse on the ups and downs of creating a strategic PR campaign for biker gangs with his tongue, no doubt, planted firmly in his cheek.[2] Or was it?

He was motivated to write on this topic by a news story carried across Canada on a wire service in mid-November 2001. The news emanated from a conference hosted by the Halifax Regional Police and the Royal Canadian Mounted Police (RCMP) to help police officers learn to deal with motorcycle gangs whose main means of support seems to be organized crime, including drug trafficking.

During that conference, a top RCMP officer was quoted in the local press as saying that these gangs are becoming 'smarter, more sophisticated and more aggressive... even hiring... public relations firms to *sanitize their image*' [emphasis added]. These biker gangs no doubt decided that their image needed a bit of cleaning up in light of the fact that they were (and continue to be) heavily publicly associated with a variety of unsavoury activities, including drug trafficking and violence. Whether or not they truly are involved in these activities didn't seem to be the issue. The issue was that they are perceived this way by the public.

Whereas it is the purview of the public relations practitioner to develop and nurture the corporate image, we can logically conclude that there are public relations 'professionals' who are willing, if not able, to provide public relations counsel to these kinds of clients. This is no joke. This is an ethical quagmire that has numerous complications and few clear answers

– because the lines over which an ethical PR practitioner dare not step are murky indeed.

THE ADVOCATE ARISES

In spite of all the potential ethical implications that readers of Dingwall's column might have considered, it all boils down to a consideration of the most ubiquitous role of the public relations field: as we discussed in this chapter, public relations practitioners are advocates for the client, organization or cause they represent. And much of that which relates to the morality of PR action emanates from this advocacy role.

As we have already established, advocacy, by definition, means promoting, supporting and defending a client, a cause, an employer. That does not mean that in the role of counsellor a public relations professional might not recommend a change in direction for that client, but fundamentally, a practitioner who continues an association with a particular client or cause implies, by association, that he or she supports what that client represents. The public has a right to this conclusion.

If, for example, you work for a pro-life group, then you are their advocate. If public support for the pro-life movement seems to be waning, a change in direction might gain favour in the arena of public opinion. But logically, you are not likely to recommend a move towards a pro-choice stance since the *raison d'être* of the organization is a particular point of view. So, if you believe in what the organization does, no matter how unethical others may see their particular stance (whether it's clear-cutting, tobacco marketing, abortion rights, cloning or even something that is illegal such as organized crime), you could make a case for the morality of your behaviour – indeed, Ku Klux Klan members believe that they are right, too. On the other hand, to the anti-smoking lobby, someone who is the public relations representative for a tobacco company is acting in a completely unethical manner. So, your professional ethics are wildly tangled up in your personal ethics. It's all a matter of choice. There's another way of looking at this issue, however.

THE 'RIGHT' TO PR COUNSEL

Newcomers to the field of PR often take the stance that a public relations practitioner is like a lawyer: everyone is entitled to legal representation. These people believe that everyone is entitled to a voice in the public media (which is difficult to argue with) and any PR practitioner with the skills could work for an organization without being morally associated with it, just as a lawyer is not morally associated with his or her client and the activities of which the client might be accused. Even clients who are believed to be guilty are entitled to a fair hearing in a democratic system. Indeed, those who subscribe to this analogy between PR and the law suggest that a PR practitioner worth his or her salt ought to be able to put those skills to work for anyone or any cause regardless of the ethics represented by that client. What nonsense. This perspective indicates a very superficial level of ethical functioning. Let's revisit this spurious analogy with lawyers that we first broached earlier in our discussions.

Lawyers represent clients, but what they are upholding in their representation is not advocacy of the individual, but advocacy of a legal system that provides for due process for everyone. This legal system has been developed over generations and provides the infrastructure for individual representation regardless of the crime. No such system exists in the arena of public communication. Thus, working for a client in whose cause you do not believe is a bit like prostitution. You're selling out your beliefs for financial gain. How sad. But it happens every day.

Client selection is but one of our ethical issues; selection of the words we use to persuade is another.

SNEAKY PROPAGANDA

With the best of intentions, PR practitioners can find themselves mired in an ethical swamp because of their use of generally accepted, and even creative, approaches to solving public relations problems. These are the insidious tactics whose ethically contentious nature is not immediately obvious to the naked eye. You need to look a bit deeper.

There's a childhood saying that you might remember: 'Sticks and stones may break my bones but words will never hurt me.' Indeed, it may have been a good way to protect ourselves from the stings of insult, but we've all grown up and we know that words can, indeed, hurt.

The vocabulary we use to create the persuasive messages can prove to be the slippery slope towards unethical behaviour.

A WAR OF WORDS

There's nothing like a war to make us take stock of the words we use and the power that they have. Given the fact that words are the fundamental tools of the public relations trade, it might be a good time to examine the ethics of the vocabularies that we use to inform, persuade and move publics to action.

'Language always one of war's first casualties' was a headline on the first page of Toronto's *Sunday Star* in the middle of March 2003, a mere four days into the latest war. Noting George Orwell's observation that war debases language, the reporter identified a slew of words that had suddenly become part of the war and media lingo, and included a rundown on the newest vocabulary from the now ubiquitous 'shock-and-awe' to 'Iraqnophobia' to 'decapitation strike'. And then there is 'collateral damage'.

As I watched the peace march in Toronto from the third floor of the HMV store in the downtown core where I was hanging out with my 14-year-old son (who had never heard of a peace march before) and picking out CDs and DVDs, I saw banners that really brought home to me the question of ethics in vocabulary: 'Children are not collateral damage', the banners screamed, and so they aren't. That's when I started thinking about the kinds of words that public relations professionals use, and even develop, and the ethics of their use.

THE PITFALLS OF EUPHEMISM

If ever there was an offensive euphemism, the term 'collateral damage' has to be one. But what is the real purpose in the application of euphemisms? And what, if anything, is wrong with using them?

Dr Kenneth Jernigan of the US Department of Education made a speech some years ago on the pitfalls of political correctness. In it, as an example, he described the evolution of one specific term. It started after the First World War as the term 'shell shock', two simple, clear syllables. This evolved after the Second World War into 'combat fatigue' – only two words but longer. Then the term mutated into a four-word term with its own acronym – PTSD or 'post-traumatic stress disorder'. As Dr Jernigan put it:

> Euphemisms and the politically correct language which they exemplify are sometimes only prissy, sometimes ridiculous, and sometimes tiresome. Often, however, they are more than that. At their worst they obscure clear thinking and damage the very people and causes they claim to benefit.[3]

The term euphemism derives from the Greek words *eu* meaning well, and *pheme*, meaning speak. *Webster's* dictionary defines the term as 'a mild or agreeable expression substituted for a realistic description of something disagreeable'.[4] It seems, then, that if we use euphemism what we are really doing is failing to use a realistic term.

I happen to agree with Dr Jernigan's characterization of euphemisms on a kind of continuum from the prissy through the ridiculous and tiresome to the obfuscation that they inevitably cause. But the motivation for creating euphemistic language is what creates a potential ethical quandary and that motivation is often grounded in pubic relations' objectives.

DOUBLESPEAK

It may be just a hair's breadth away from the innocuous euphemism, but doublespeak, by its very definition, is language that is created to be evasive and just ambiguous enough that it may intentionally lead to confusion or, at its worst, deception. It is this area of a deliberate attempt to deceive or even simply confuse where the invention of new words or phrases crosses the line from the merely annoying to the downright immoral.

As William Lutz, an English professor at Rutgers and author of the book *The New Doublespeak: Why no one knows what anyone's saying anymore*, suggests, doublespeak actually only pretends to say something:

> Doublespeak comes in many forms, from the popular buzzwords that everyone uses but no one really understands – 'glocalization,' 'competitive dynamics,' 're-equitizing' and 'empowerment' – to language that tries to hide meaning: 're-engineering,' 'synergy,' 'adjustment,' 'restructure' and 'force management program.'[5]

It's one thing to use euphemistic language in an honest attempt to avoid insulting someone (à la political correctness – a separate issue unto itself), and ethically quite another to intentionally attempt to obfuscate by use of terms that have no precisely agreed-upon meaning. Doing so puts the PR practitioner farther and farther into the propaganda swamp.

Indeed, 'made-up' words tell only part of the story of doublespeak. There's a far more insidious and perhaps even more ethically treacherous strategy.

THE 'CONTROLLED LEXICON'

Public relations practitioners are often geniuses in this domain. We create specific messages to target specific publics and choose our words carefully. None of this is inherently problematic from a moral standpoint, but when the control of the allowable vocabulary results in obfuscation of the truth, this is when potential ethical problems arise.

Consider the situation described by authors Sheldon Rampton and John Stauber in their recent book *Trust Us, We're Experts: How industry manipulates science and gambles with your future*. They tell the story of a November 1996 presentation at a PR conference by a PR executive, one of whose assignments involved managing the image of Nutrasweet™, Monsanto's artificial sweetener.

According to Rampton and Stauber, this PR executive described a PR strategy that recognized that words such as 'artificial' (as in artificial sweetener, which even the company says it is) suggested negative images to consumers and set about removing them from all references to the product. He is quoted by Rampton and Stauber as saying 'Words such as "substitute," "artificial," "chemical," "laboratory," "scientist" were removed forever from our lexicon and replaced with words such as "discovered," "choice," "variety," "unique," "different," "new taste".'[6]

Are any of these words immoral in themselves? Of course not, but when you examine the situation in this kind of black and white way, it's not hard to understand why consumers have a difficult time trusting manufacturers and their PR campaigns.

THE VOCABULARY OF PUBLIC RELATIONS

Andy Green, author of *Creativity in Public Relations*, seems to suggest that we need to create new vocabulary so that public relations professionals don't have to resort to inflating 'the significance of a small part of a situation', or masking or obscuring 'the situation with a distraction', both of which he admits leave PR open to accusations of lying, a conclusion that is difficult to argue with. In Green's view, however, 'The way for our profession to constructively debate and manage these issues is to extend our vocabulary – rather than be constrained by black-and-white definitions of telling the truth.'[7]

We can infer from Green's stated view that he is suggesting that public relations practitioners should take a proactive approach to finding new words in an effort to avoid the public perception that we are lying. This is a troublesome perspective; creating a new vocabulary, presumably with meanings that we as a profession assign for the purpose of avoiding the label 'liar', is what some would refer to as 'bullsh*t'.

In her book *Your Call is Important to Us: The truth about bullsh*t*, author Laura Penny puts forward her thesis that bullsh*t is a growth industry of the information age and that 'the most prolific producers of bullsh*t [are] advertising and public relations'.[8] I'm certain Rampton and Stauber (*Trust Us We're Experts!*) would agree heartily. And in spite of Penny's obviously cynical, self-righteous stance, it's hard to ignore the fact that although she may not have the full picture of what public relations does, her perception does have that ring of truth in many instances. Penny never does define B-S, though. For that we have to look to a somewhat more sagacious source.

Professor Harry Frankfurt is a renowned moral philosopher and professor emeritus at Princeton University. He wrote a paper some years ago on the very subject of B-S. In 2005 it was republished as a tiny, hard-backed book titled *On Bullsh*t*. He, too considers advertising and public relations, along with politics, to be 'replete with instances of bullsh*t so unmitigated that they can serve among the most indisputable and classic paradigms of the concept'.[9] Frankfurt's discussion of the subject is a bit more useful for us in practice since he comes as close to a definition of the concept as anyone. He considers the real meaning of bullsh*t to be that it is 'grounded neither in a belief that is true, nor as a lie must be, in a belief that it is not true. It is just this lack of connection to a concern with the truth – this indifference to how things really are' that he regards as the 'essence' of B-S.[10] As public relations practitioners who are committed to integrity and truth in public communication, we need to be concerned about a real and perceived indifference to the truth. This is the slippery slope.

As we discussed earlier, when we were children we may have thought that sticks and stones can break our bones but names will never hurt us, and perhaps it worked to preserve our self-esteem in the face of word-wielding bullies. Times, however, have changed. We're grown-ups now and words can, indeed, hurt. As Lord Byron wrote, 'But words are things, and a small drop of ink, falling like dew, upon a thought, produces that which makes thousands, perhaps millions, think.' We have the power to make millions of people think about specific things in specific ways; we have a responsibility to ensure that we do so without harming the public or our own reputations.

PERSUASION BY LOBBY

And while we're considering the issue of our power to make people think about specific things in specific ways, we need to discuss that revered lobby technique that public relations professionals often employ in an attempt to persuade particular groups – notably government – to their point of view.

In his book *A Social History of Spin*, Stuart Ewan makes a compelling case for all the world to read that the PR industry steers the public mind, and by doing so undermines the very meaning of democratic principles. And although much of what the average PR person does at his or her desk on a day-to-day basis seems far removed from these earth-changing events, the more high-profile and often creative approaches to strategic public relations do, indeed, require an imaginative strategy that may cross the line into the murky area of manipulation.

One example of such a creative strategy is what places like the PR Watch [www.prwatch.org], a kind of watchdog on the PR industry, call front groups. As new and creative as this approach might seem, it actually has a rather long and not altogether sparkling history.

In the 1930s, public relations pioneer Carl Byoir, a contemporary of Edward Bernays, was holding his own in the arena of developing new and original strategies to solve corporate communications dilemmas. As if his work as a front man for both the Cuban dictatorship and the German Tourist Information Office hadn't muddied his reputation enough, he went to work back home in the United States for grocery giant A & P. Although the actual facts of the story vary depending upon which source you read (the PR Museum [www.prmuseum.com] seems to present it as a legitimate lobby), Carl Byoir is credited with developing the first front group as a PR ploy.

When proposed taxation on chain stores threatened to close down his client's operation, he advised them to go down fighting. His strategy involved setting up what some sources indicate were in fact dummy organizations such as the National Consumers' Tax Commission and Business Property Owners Inc. to do what we might now call indirect lobbying against the tax.[11] To all appearances, these groups were grass-roots organizations echoing the opinions of an often silent majority in a democratic society. At what point, then, does the front group overstep the boundaries of ethics? When is a front group manipulation and when is it simply a good strategy?

TRANSPARENCY VERSUS OBFUSCATION

PR Watch (PRW) has what they call a rogue's gallery of front groups. First, there's ActivistCash.com which, according to its website, 'root[s] out the funding sources of the most notorious anti-consumer groups'.[12] PRW contends that it is actually run by a Washington lobbyist, and while claiming to expose the hidden funding behind these environmental and health activist groups, refuses to disclose its own resources. According to PRW, ActivistCash is funded by the tobacco, alcohol and restaurant industries.

Then there's the recently deactivated Global Climate Coalition, which evidently has successfully completed its job of 'contributing to a new national approach to global warming'.[13] According to PRW, it was sponsored by the auto, oil, coal and other such industries with a mandate to lead you to believe that global warming isn't really a problem at all.

These kinds of front groups have a clear ethical dilemma in the area of disclosure. Is it ethical to lobby for a particular point of view or to persuade people to think and act differently without allowing your target public to have basic information on the lobby group – who you are and where your money comes from? If this lack of transparency in any way misleads the audience, the answer has to be no. But where do we draw the line?

Surely, there are some groups such as those dedicated to health-related issues that are ethical public relations tools for their financial backers. Frequently, though, their sponsors are all pharmaceutical and healthcare companies that stand to benefit from exposure of their name and logo to potential consumers. Does this make them unethical if they are clear about their sources of income? Perhaps less so than those that are not, but they are dipping at least a toe into the waters of ethical quandaries.

If we use the test of disclosure, then the answer is no – this is clearly an ethical public relations approach to enhancing the image of the drug companies. However, not all such organizations clearly indicate to their publics – especially those targeted to lay audiences – that they are, in fact, front groups for drug companies. They purport to be in the business of patient education. This could hardly be considered an impartial source of treatment information for a vulnerable public such as patients. This kind of organization falls into that twilight zone of ethical murkiness.

The bottom line is that there is considerable opportunity for public relations professionals to be more innovative in their approaches to solving PR problems or capitalizing on PR opportunities. But in the heat of the creative process, we cannot afford to lose sight of the potential ethical quagmires into which we may be falling.

Notes

1. Larson, C (1973) *Persuasion, Reception and Responsibility*, Wadsworth, Belmont, CA
2. Dingwall, J [accessed 14 October 2003] PR for Biker Gangs: The Opportunity from Heck. http://www.prcanada.ca/TRADECRAFT/GANGT.HTM
3. Jernigan, Kenneth [accessed 19 March 2003] The Pitfalls of Political Correctness. Copyright National Federation of the Blind. http://www.blind.net/bpg00005.htm
4. *Webster's New Illustrated Dictionary of the English Language* (1992), PMC Publishing Company, Inc, New York, p 336
5. Lutz, William [accessed 16 October 2003] Life Under the Chief Doublespeak Officer. http://www.dt.org/html/Doublespeak.html
6. Rampton, S and Stauber, J (2001) *Trust Us, We're Experts!: How industry manipulates science and gambles with your future*, Jeremy P Tarcher, New York, pp 65–66
7. Green, Andy [accessed 23 January 2003] The Need to Create a New Vocabulary for the PR Profession. www.prsi.org/_Publications/magazines/Tactics/0301views1.html
8. Penny, L (2005) *Your Call Is Important to Us: The truth about bullsh*t*, McLelland & Stewart, Toronto, pp 3–4
9. Frankfurt, H (2005) *On Bullsh*t*, Princeton University Press, Princeton, NJ, p 22

10. Frankfurt, Ibid, pp 33–34
11. Bleifuss, J (1994) Flack attack, *Utne Reader,* January–February, pp 72–73, 76–77
12. ActivistCash website [accessed 16 October 2003]. http://www.activistcash.com
13. Global Climate Coalition website [accessed 16 October 2003]. http://www.globalclimate.org

13

Good causes and bad taste

What is exhilarating in bad taste is the aristocratic pleasure of giving offence.
Charles Baudelaire

Public relations' role with respect to the marketing function of the organization gives rise to a number of specific ethical issues. These issues arise when the marketing of products and services uses specific tactics: first, marketing on the coat-tails of so-called 'good causes', and second, the even more nebulous issue of tastefulness or lack thereof.

In our continuing journey through the ethical quagmire created by PR strategies and the moral dilemmas that can spring from them we need to discuss these marketing-related tactics.

'AWARE' OF THE ISSUES

Every year we make it through one of them after another. I refer to those ubiquitous 'awareness' months (or occasionally weeks) – organ donor awareness, diabetes awareness, volunteer awareness, kidney disease awareness, to name but a very few. My personal favourite, and clearly a favourite among those corporations seeking to spend their strategic philanthropy budget, is breast cancer awareness month. Let's use breast cancer awareness as an example of a cause as we discuss the ethics of public relations campaigns hooked to the coat-tails of good causes.

Before we embark on this discussion, I feel the need to provide full disclosure. I do not have breast cancer. However, before you begin to draw conclusions, you also need to know that both my mother and my sister had breast cancer. So, I suppose that I might develop it some day, too. But then so might many other women, since the main risk factor in the development of this disease is being a woman. That said, you need to know that I feel no particular compulsion to 'run for the cure', to 'cook for the cure', or any of the other activities that are designed to enhance the image of organizations – from banks to vacuum cleaner manufacturers – that have pinned pink ribbons to their products, services and employees.

Cause-related marketing and strategic philanthropy programmes are bedrock public relations tools with enormous capacities to develop mutually beneficial outcomes for both the sponsoring organization and the cause being supported. 'Good causes' are usually in desperate need of support from the profit-minded sector and profit-minded organizations need to enhance the communities in which they function. So, it seems like a marriage made in heaven. But are there any ethical lines that need to be considered in the strategic decision-making about which causes to support? I believe that there are – however, they are murky and fraught with controversy. Breast cancer is only one of a number of what appear to be clearly good causes that might be less clear on second thought.

A STAPLE OF COMMUNITY RELATIONS

Before we discuss the ethical issues involved, it might be a good idea to ensure that we all have the same understanding of these community relations tools and tactics that are so popular in strategies designed to enhance relationships between organizations and their communities. What could be a more noble objective than to give back to the community?

The term *strategic philanthropy* is now widely used to identify a profit-making organization's strategic public relations approach in support of community activities. Here the term 'community' can refer to the local, regional, national or even international community depending on the organization's reach. The strategic objective from a public relations point of view is to maximize the image-building and relationship-enhancing aspects of the donation or sponsorship by finding a cause that can accomplish this objective.

Cause-related marketing, often confused by marketers with social marketing, is the tactic that identifies an organization's products or services with a specific social cause. For example, if a brewery creates a campaign against drinking and driving, they are marketing their beer by relating it to a social cause – the cause is forwarded, but the bottom line is increasing market share. *Social marketing*, by contrast and by definition, is a campaign created (usually by an organization devoted to the cause) for the sole purpose of selling the cause (or behaviour change), with no hidden agenda of selling products. Social marketing uses the techniques and tactics traditionally used to market products and services to market ideas. If a condom manufacturer sponsors and develops a public communication campaign to promote safer sex, they are doing cause-related marketing. On the other hand, if the regional non-profit AIDS coalition develops a marketing campaign to promote safer sex, that's social marketing. The primary purpose of a social marketing campaign is to 'influence individuals' behavior [sic] to improve their well-being and that of society.'[1]

Whereas it seems like a truly good thing for profit-minded organizations to give back to their communities, there are some issues that are often not considered, or quickly discarded as irrelevant, by the public relations professionals engaged in finding the best way both to promote the organization as community-minded and truly make a difference. These two issues of mutuality often conflict.

SEEKING A GOOD FIT

There is little doubt that the eradication of a disease such as breast cancer is a noble cause to support. Who wouldn't want to be associated with the cure for such a devastating illness? But before you run out and wrap pink ribbons around your products and services like CIBC, Kitchenaid, Betty Crocker, Swarovski, Hush Puppies, Ernst & Young, Tetley Tea and Wonderbra (a good fit if ever I saw one) to name only a few (to see more examples of this you could visit the Canadian Breast Cancer Foundation's website [www.cbcf.org]), perhaps a few sobering thoughts about what you are actually supporting would be worthwhile. If all you're looking for is a high-profile cause, you won't need to ask any more questions since breast cancer clearly fits the bill, but if you're actually interested in making a difference in your community, there are a few questions that need answers.

If your organization is seeking to support a high-risk women's health cause, you might do a bit of initial research. You will discover that it is not breast cancer that is the top killer of women in developed countries, rather it is heart disease. However, breast cancer seems to be much more high profile and emotionally charged. Perhaps the emotional charge is related to the body part, or our collective perception of the body part that is affected by the disease.

With that in mind we might consider a *San Francisco Chronicle* newspaper column[2] that introduced me to the San Francisco-based advocacy group Breast Cancer Action whose motto is 'think before you pink'. It is their contention that breast cancer today is big business and that many organizations are forming marketing attachments to the cause while really donating very little towards a cure. For example, the high-profile American breast cancer group Susan G. Komen Foundation recently spent $26 million on research, $6 million on treatment and a whopping $33 million (all in US dollars) on public education, much of which is devoted to teaching breast self-examination (which recent medical research has indicated to be far less useful than first hoped).

Even the Canadian Breast Cancer Foundation, which every year is the recipient of the 'run for the cure' money that is donated by individuals and corporate entities, one year spent only 59 per cent of its money on research.[3] And my money, if it isn't going into research, it isn't going towards a 'cure.' At least in the United Kingdom the organization that sponsors the Breast Cancer Awareness month and pins pink ribbons on products of organizations that support them calls itself 'Breast Cancer Care' and the money goes to a range of services for women with breast cancer. There is no perception that your donation will cure anything.

Supporting causes or big business?

There seems to be a growing subculture of writers who believe that breast cancer activists and all of those women who participate religiously in many of the high-profile fund raisers for breast cancer research might just be cogs in the wheels of big businesses for whom breast cancer is lucrative indeed. According to Judy Brady writing for the Breast Cancer Action newsletter, few people seem to know that breast cancer awareness month is what she describes as 'a slick public relations campaign designed by Zeneca's once-parent company Imperial Chemical Industries'.[4] Zeneca is the pharmaceutical company that produces tamoxifen, a chemotherapy agent used both for treating patients with breast cancer and for prevention in high-risk women.

So, what is this all about and where are the ethical issues (if they are not already painfully evident)? When public relations practitioners are making strategic decisions about which community causes to align their organizations with, from an ethical standpoint, it is important to determine the benefit not only to the organization, but to the community as well. Indeed, it's critical that, to be an ethical public relations strategy, it must not in any way mislead the public. The actual impact of the contribution should not be overblown and the target activities for the support need to be clear and not overshadowed by media hype. You'd better do your research.

There is a great deal of public cynicism about the social cause activities of profit-minded organizations these days. Whereas there is nothing fundamentally immoral or evil about polishing your organization's image in association with community-mindedness, there is a requirement for honesty. No one really expects that there will be total altruism in an organization's community activities. However, what is important to the ethical practice of public relations is that there be mutual benefit to both the organization and the cause, and that the promotion be honest.

After taking a heartfelt look at these ethical issues, if breast cancer 'awareness' is still where you believe your money is best spent for the community – then it's the right decision. Given my own family background, I'd be the first in line to support finding a cure – but more awareness? I don't think so. Besides, I'm told that there are more people employed in the cancer business today than there are people with the disease – and the morbidity statistics are only getting worse.

Now we'll move on to our second discussion of public relations and marketing tactics that need further scrutiny.

FROM GOOD CAUSES TO GOOD TASTE

Have you ever seen an advertisement, read a political cartoon or read a so-called funny story in a newsletter only to have your immediate reaction be: that's in poor taste? You know the feeling – it's not based on any objective analysis, rather on a gut-level, personal reaction to the content or delivery, or both. Occasionally, tenets of so-called political correctness provide a touchstone for evaluation, but more often than not it's just a feeling.

How do you know when something is in bad taste? And, more to the point, is tastefulness (or lack thereof) ever an ethical issue?

We need to start by defining 'good taste'. Most newspapers and magazines, for example, indicate that advertising or other matter for their publications must be in good taste, but it's rare to find an actual definition of what this means. If these organizations are asked who will define such a thing, the usual response is that they will. In other words, the definition of what is in good taste is a relative thing and changes depending on the circumstances.

Several years ago, clothing manufacturer Benetton ran yet another series of controversial ads. For a sweater manufacturer, they have ventured into seemingly incongruent areas. Through the years they've used AIDS, violence, terrorism, and more recently, death-row inmates in their advertising. Many dissenters believe that these latter ads stepped over the line of good taste. However, editor Rogier van Bakel wrote in Advertising Age's *Creativity* magazine:

> You want to 'lift society to a higher level'? Go work for PBS... Advertising is a mirror. In a culture where extreme snarkiness [sic], even crudeness, has become a dominant tone (Eminem, Maxim, Tom Green, the Farrelly Brothers), it's no surprise that admakers listen, and reflect what they hear.[5]

So it seems that (a) there is a fine line between good and bad taste, (b) good taste is at least somewhat related to personal preference, and (c) the line between tastefulness and tastelessness is difficult to discern. This is analogous to that black line through a grey area that characterizes ethical dilemmas. But for those of us engaged in the business of public communication, it's important to consider when that line should not be crossed.

Crossing the line from questionable taste to bad taste sometimes takes us into a moral dilemma. Up to that point, it's only a question of the kind of image you want to convey. Beyond that, it's a question of right and wrong.

Tastelessness and harm

A few years ago the Spanish branch of Greenpeace embarked on a unique communications strategy – unique at least in their industry. Their objective was to raise money by using a desk diary which was what *The Sunday Times* described as 'sexy'. According to press reports, the diary featured nude models lounging in environmentally related situations. For example, one apparently was caught by the camera as she lounged naked on empty mineral water bottles, evidently to highlight the pitfalls of non-recyclable items.

Not surprisingly, feminist groups were outraged that such a group as Greenpeace would resort to what they judged to be sexist advertising. So, is this a question of good taste versus bad taste, or is it that *and* something more?

First, whether images of naked women are used to sell environmental issues rather than sex seems a moot point. *What* they are selling is immaterial. *How* they are selling it is what is germane to the discussion.

Clearly, you as an individual will have an opinion on this subject from a purely stylistic point of view. Either you will consider this to be in good taste or in bad. For the sake of argument, let's say that you consider this to be a tasteless way of gaining public attention. The further question is whether or not it constitutes an unethical way of promoting issues.

If we use the test of whether or not the approach harms anyone, then it is, indeed, moving into ethically treacherous territory. There is little doubt that the feminist groups, as well as many individual women, will feel that such an approach to fund-raising is harming women – their ability to be taken seriously, their opportunities for equality etc. After all, there were evidently no nude men in the diary – at least none were mentioned!

When public relations practitioners (and marketers) are developing strategies for achieving communication and relationship objectives, they consider the potential efficiency and effectiveness of the chosen approach. It's equally important to consider the potential ethical implications beyond the question of good taste. To help you make ethical choices in support of good causes, consider the questions in Figure 13.1.

Questions to assess the ethics of selecting good causes

1. Is it a legitimate cause in need of our support?

2. Will our support of their cause truly be of benefit to the community?

3. Is the cause congruent with our mission and philosophy?

4. Are our employees likely to feel positively disposed to the cause?

5. Will we be able to enhance our image without appearing opportunistic?

6. Will the publicity surrounding our relationship with this cause be tasteful?

7. Will our support of this cause be offensive to anyone?

8. Does the good that is likely to come from our support outweigh any negative perceptions?

Figure 13.1 *Questions to assess the ethics of selecting good causes*

Picasso is quoted as saying: 'Ah, good taste! What a dreadful thing! Taste is the enemy of creativeness.' He, however, was a fine artist. The difference between an artist and a communicator is that as communicators, unlike artists, we *do* need to be concerned about how people will respond to our messages.

Notes

1. Social Marketing Institute [accessed 23 October 2003] – What is it? http://www.social-marketing.org/aboutus.html

2. Ryan, Joan [accessed 16 October 2003] Cures Not Campaigns (originally published in the *San Francisco Chronicle*, 22 October 2002). http://www.susanlovemd.org/community/great reads/021022.html

3. Canadian Breast Cancer Foundation [accessed 23 October 2003] Annual Report 2002, p 28. http://www.cbcf.org/pdfs/CBCF2002 AR.pdf
4. Brady, Judy [accessed 23 October 2003] Public Relations and Cancer, Breast Cancer Awareness Newsletter #50 (October/November, 1998). http://www.bcaction.org/Pages/SearchablePages/1998Newsletters /Newsletter050F.html
5. Van Bakel, Rogier [accessed 6 June 2002] Do the Taste Test, *Creativity* magazine. www.ecreativesearch.com/news/01-05-18/cre-test.asp

14

Authorship and deception

Copy from one, it's plagiarism; copy from two, it's research.
Wilson Mizner (1876–1933)

Sometimes people outside the field of public relations have difficulty understanding just exactly what we do. This is largely because we do most of our work behind the scenes. Then, when they do have an opportunity to learn more about the less-high-profile aspects, they often misinterpret our actions and our motives. Sometimes, however, even within our field we need to consider more deeply how we come to justify widely accepted practices.

A PR PRACTICE

New York Times' columnist Randy Cohen has for many years written a column now titled 'The ethicist'. A self-described 'accidental ethicist', he says in the introduction to his book *The Good, the Bad and the Difference,* that he has no actual credentials in the field of ethics.[1] Nevertheless, he pens a regular column on everyday ethics and people read it and listen to his regular podcasts, available on the online version of the *New York Times*. So his opinion on ethical matters seems to have influence. That's why when he writes a column with 'PR' in the title, we should perhaps pay attention.

In 2003 he received a letter from a reader who wrote that he was considering hiring a PR 'representative' to help him promote his new business but was concerned about the PR person writing letters for him – essentially ghost-writing – with his name signed to them. The reader asked if this might not be lying.

This seems like a rather familiar scenario in public relations offices across North America and probably around the world. Every day we write speeches, memos, annual report letters, product and service marketing letters and so much more for the employers and clients who have hired us to help them with their communication challenges. They have hired us because we possess the skills that they lack.

Cohen's response was to advise us that 'context is all'. He suggests that when the president of the United States gives a speech, the public assumes that the words are not his own specifically, rather written by a speech writer and that this is acceptable because the public knows this. I'm not sure from where he derived this conclusion, but I'm not as certain as Cohen is that most people in a democratic society really do realize that political speeches are often (usually) written by professional speech writers – public relations people.

Notwithstanding his possibly inaccurate conclusion here, Cohen goes on to suggest that when someone's name appears on such things as novels, magazine articles or op-ed pieces, the assumption is that the person actually penned the words; thus for another person's name to appear is, in fact, lying. To follow this line of reasoning further, we could assume that anyone who has ever hired a ghost writer is essentially lying to the public. That would probably come as quite a surprise to all those celebrities, sports stars and political heavyweights who hired writers to pen their memoirs. I don't think that it ever occurred to them that they were putting their signatures to anything but their own thoughts expressed in such a way that people might actually read them. Indeed, their readers may or may not realize that the books have been ghost written, but they still recognize that the ideas came from the subject of the book. We need to explore the concepts of plagiarising and 'ghosting' a bit further.

THE UNSEEN AUTHOR

Plagiarism is a term we tend to think about most often in terms of college or university essays, and lately in journalism. We are exhorted from early on in our careers as 'paper writers' to refrain from such behaviour at all costs or suffer the academic consequences. Students, however, often have difficulty understanding what the term really means and exactly how to avoid it. Indeed, it seems it is not so clear to business people, either.

The *Compact Oxford English Dictionary* defines the verb 'to plagiarize' as follows: 'to take (the work or idea of someone else) and pass it off as one's own'.[2]

The word derives from the Latin *plagiarius*, which means 'kidnapper', and from the Greek *plagion* meaning 'a kidnapping'. Other definitions offer more insight that provides further clarification on whether or not the way we 'pass off' work in the practice of public relations may or may not be unethical.

For example, the Modern Languages Association (MLA) defines plagiarism as using another person's ideas or work without giving credit.[3] The MLA further suggests that much plagiarism is unintentional and the result of sloppy research; this, however does not apply in the PR situations to which we refer.

The American Psychological Association, purveyors of research paper presentation style for many college and university departments, provides a similar discussion:

> an author does not present the work of another as if it were his or her own work. This can extend to ideas as well as written words... [A]n author may not know where an idea for a study originated. If the author does know, however, the author should acknowledge the source; this includes personal communications.[4]

Again, there is the exhortation to provide identification of sources. Another characteristic that is generally held to be a part of defining plagiarism in practice is captured by the definition provided by the online source *Infoplease*. It defines plagiarism as 'the unauthorized use or close imitation of the language and thoughts of another author and the representation of them as one's own original work'.[5] This practical addition of the term 'unauthorized' begins to bring us closer to an understanding of whether or not PR does, indeed, resort to plagiarism. When a public relations practitioner is hired by an individual or organization to express that client's message and then provides 'work-for-hire' as part of the service, the use of the words is clearly 'authorized', and in addition is expressing not the ideas and creations of the writer but those of the person hiring the writer. This seems clearly within the bounds of ethical behaviour, and in fact the person using the words isn't the PR person at all: it is the person hiring the writer to produce the media release, article, speech or book, for example. And this is not plagiarism in the strictest sense; it constitutes what has come to be called 'ghost-writing'. In this case the words are neither unacknowledged – at least not privately – nor unauthorized. Ghost-writing, though, does beg fuller discussion.

CROSSING THE LINE?

One day I received an e-mail from a former student who had just finished reading the book *Ghosting: A double life* by Jennie Erdal, which describes the author's relationship with a British media mogul.[6] According to this tell-all tome, Erdal had been hired to write everything from her employer's novels and interviews to his love letters. Her title was 'editor.' My student was transported back to our ethics classes and she posed two potential dilemmas:

- What are the ethics of 'ghosting' in the first place?
- What are the ethics of revealing such a role?

The exploration of the answers to these two questions helps us to understand the ethics of our penchant for writing-for-hire. This activity takes up a significant amount of time in the working day of many public relations practitioners, so feeling comfortable with its ethics is important. We'll use Erdal's experience as an illustrative case.

The author of *Ghosting*, Jennie Erdal, evidently spent some 20 years as the ghost writer for a flamboyant London publisher who wanted to be a published novelist, among other things. Not only did she ghostwrite for her employer, but she then went on to actually reveal this publicly. 'Ghost writers don't usually reveal themselves; invisibility is implicit in the bargains they make', says author Joyce Johnson on the back cover of Erdal's book.[7] Is this kind of revelation the crux of the ethical questions for those who write for hire? Or is the ethical question implicit in the work itself?

In the book, Erdal characterizes her work as using her skills as a writer to help her client express his thoughts in a way that he was not able to do. Isn't that what professional public relations writers do, are expected to do and are paid to do? Is what we are doing unethical? The short answer is no – and yes.

Just as with many of the bedrock tools and tactics we use to help our clients and employers deal with their public relations issues, writing for others under someone else's byline is fraught with often undiscovered ethical traps. There are some ethical principles that we might consider before we examine instances of ghosting that are considered appropriate – as well as some that are not.

As we have previously established, the primary ethical principle to consider when trying to determine the 'rightness' or 'wrongness' of an action is non-maleficence – to do no harm. Any activity that potentially harms others needs to be justified on the basis of other competing principles. Ghostwriting in and of itself does no harm; only to the extent that it might transgress other principles might it turn out to have ethical problems.

One of the other principles we hold dear in the field of public relations and that it could transgress is truth telling. As we have discussed in earlier chapters, codes of ethics for our profession as well as generally held conventions about deception and truth in public communication direct us to always do our best to be truthful in our messaging – both in content and in delivery, both of which have an impact on how our messages are perceived. For example, if the way a message is delivered is truthful in its content but misleading in its delivery, then it can be considered to be deceptive. Is ghosting deceptive? Some instances of ghostwriting are; others are not likely to be considered as lies.

Maintaining the confidentiality of employers and clients is another aspect of ethical public relations that needs to be considered in judging the morality of this activity. By its very definition, ghostwriting describes a confidential relationship between writer and employer, at least on the part of the writer. The person buying the writing and whose actual name appears on it is also buying privacy and is the only party who has the right to disclose that the material is ghostwritten; the reasonable expectation of the employer is that the ghost will remain hidden from view. Because of its very nature, the notion of transparency is not a part of the ghostwriting business.

ACCEPTABLE VERSUS UNACCEPTABLE USES

While there are truly many controversies and opinions on the issues, there are several places where ghostwriting is considered acceptable and even expected.

The first, and an area where most of us will never tread, is the celebrity autobiography. Many (perhaps even most) celebrities, and this includes everyone from Hollywood stars to politicians, hire ghostwriters. Perhaps it's the smart ones who do. These are the ones who recognize that they do not possess the writing skills necessary to communicate their ideas in this form. That's where expert ghostwriters come in. Is there deception here? It is clear that the story told is the one coming from the one whose name will actually appear on the cover of the book. That much is true and the readers usually don't much care whether or not the actor or politician actually did the writing – in fact, many readers would say that they fully expected that the book would be written by someone else. It's accepted, conventional practice.

Speeches are another area where ghosting is probably more the norm than the exception, and it is an important area of PR writing. Is writing a speech that will be delivered by someone else deceptive in any way? Again this is one of those areas where most people don't necessarily believe that the politician at the podium actually wrote the speech, although clearly some still do – but the audience does have a right to expect that it reflects the speaker's true beliefs and that it was reviewed by him or her prior to its delivery. We'll explore this a bit more later in the section.

Because they are the expert writers in the organization, public relations professionals often write opinion/editorial pieces for their CEOs or others in their organization whose bylines will appear in the newspaper. This is one area that is very controversial when it comes to the ethics of ghosting. Some editors of magazines and newspapers have declared that ghost-written opinion pieces are in their view dishonest. An ethical PR person hired to write an op/ed piece under someone else's byline will agree to assist in the writing, but not to ghost write it entirely. Polishing someone else's prose is an acceptable practice.

One area where ghosting is considered completely unacceptable is in academic writing. Scholars submitting papers to academic journals are expected to have written them (even if there are eight such authors listed). No ghostwriters are welcome. The medical profession refers to it as the 'ethics of authorship'. Academic medicine has been grappling with this issue perhaps even more than others because of their relationship with drug companies who do employ writers. The World Association of Medical Editors guidelines are very specific in saying that ghosting is dishonest and unacceptable,[8] an important consideration for PR writers who write for pharmaceutical companies. This kind of guideline makes the authorship very transparent. Their approach provides some assistance to the rest of us who are looking for ways to be able to use professional writers while at the same time avoiding the possibility of deception.

When it comes to things like love letters, though, which Erdal says she wrote for her employer, it seems that the receiver would expect that they would actually be written by the sender and that there would be some measure of privacy about them. A third party's input might not be welcome. It is certainly not clear cut, although I'll venture an opinion that this is an unacceptable form of ghosting!

Generally, passing off someone else's work as your own is considered to be plagiarism at best. However, when it comes to the work-for-hire issue, it is considered acceptable. If you are hired to do a job, then the work you do belongs to the person who hired you (an important concept for PR people who write a great deal for employers – the work does not belong to you, the employee, unless you have a contract that stipulates such). Whether or not the ideas communicated are those of the sender is another issue.

The revelation of one's role as a ghostwriter later is another issue altogether. There is usually a reasonable expectation that a ghost writer will always stay in the background, but there may be circumstances that require such a revelation. In the case of Jennie Erdal, motivations are important here. If her revelation was purely for her own gain, then I believe that she has breached a confidence and has made an ethical transgression. This would be the same if her motive were to discredit the person for whom she wrote. As a result of the increasingly ubiquitous nature of speech-writing, however, the writer often, with permission, uses the speeches that he or she has written as part of a professional portfolio. In this case, there is clearly no attempt to suggest that the person who delivered the speech actually penned it.

Finally we should consider what outside observers – such as Mr Cohen – might think. He clearly concludes that there is something inherently unethical about the plagiarism/ghostwriting tactic, although his perspective might be an anachronism of sorts. Back in 1961, a young American professor of speech communication provided a very similar point of view on the subject. Now a professor emeritus at the University of Minnesota, Ernest Bormann wrote the following passage in an article about the ethics of ghostwriting:

> it does no good to argue that deception is not involved in ghostwriting because the speaker endorses the ideas by delivering them, or because everybody knows that the speeches are ghostwritten anyway. Everyone does not know... [T]hose who may believe it of public men they dislike still like to keep the fiction that their candidate writes his own speeches.[9]

Prof Bormann goes on to provide erudite ethical justification for ghostwriting from a variety of eminent thinkers and yet concludes that although ghostwriting might be inevitable and perhaps even expected, these characteristics do not provide ethical justification. Times, it seems, have changed, as have the ethical conventions.

The bottom line seems to be that any attempt to cover the true source of the thoughts and ideas (such as in the new problems associated with blogging and the use of front groups) is the kind of ethical treachery that should be avoided by the concerned PR practitioner. It harms our publics, our profession and eventually our careers.

Notes

1.   Cohen, R (2002) *The Good, the Bad and the Difference: How to tell right from wrong in everyday situations*, Doubleday, New York

2. *Compact Oxford English Dictionary* [accessed 4 December 2007] http://www.askoxford.com/concise_oed/plagiarize?view=uk

3. Gibaldi, J and Achtert, W (1988) *MLA Handbook for Writers for Research Papers*, 3rd edn, The Modern Language Association of America, New York

4. American Psychological Association. (2001) *Publication Manual of the APA*, 5th edn, APA, Washington, DC

5. Infoplease online dictionary [accessed 4 December 2007] http://www.infoplease.com/ ipd/A0590972.html

6. Erdal, J (2004) *Ghosting: A double life*, Canongate Books Ltd, Edinburgh

7. Erdal, Ibid

8. World Association of Medical Editors [accessed 4 December 2007] Ghostwriting initiated by commercial companies, WAME Guidelines, http://www.wame.org/resources/policies#ghost

9. Bormann, E (1961) Ethics of ghostwritten speeches, *Quarterly Journal of Speech*, **42** (3), pp 262–267

Part 4

Organizations, ethics and public relations

When you finally come right down to it, everyday ethics in public relations is really a matter of being able first to recognize when you are faced with an ethical dilemma (what we've been talking about until now), and then make an ethically defensible decision about your behaviour in the situation. If your role within your organization is more strategic and you truly take on the role of public relations counsellor, then your decision may be even more critical, since you may need to help the organization make ethical decisions that affect both their bottom line and their reputation. In this next part, the final one, we'll explore how ethical decisions are actually made. In addition, we need to come full circle to where we started – the issue of what is the true foundation for our concern about ethics in the everyday practice of public relations. That foundation lies within the context of social responsibility. We define social responsibility and explore what role, if any, public relations plays in an organization's overall ethics strategy.

Finally, we'll look to the future, towards the new breed of PR practitioners who are sitting in today's college and university classrooms. Are they really learning anything about ethical public relations and, perhaps even more important, what will they be able to teach the rest of us?

15

The true reality of everyday ethics: making decisions

A decision without the pressure of consequence is hardly a decision at all.

Eric Langmuir

This is probably the chapter you've been waiting for as you've moved through the previous discussions which have focused more on the underlying ethical principles and your own approach to ethical thinking. After all, the heart of ethics in practice is facing those everyday ethical dilemmas and making decisions that you can live with. However, before you can examine ethical decision-making and apply those principles to your own public relations practice, you do need a bit of background work. Now, though, we have finally arrived at that point where we can really get to the substance of ethics in PR practice.

We make decisions every day of our lives. When I teach classes on the public relations process – which in itself is nothing more than a systematic way for making and implementing decisions – I always remind students that the very fact that they are sitting in that classroom is testament to the fact that they have made myriad decisions even in the short time since they got out of bed that morning. They decided what to wear, whether or not to eat breakfast and what to have, if anything, whether to come to class or not, how to get there, where to sit, to whom they would speak and the list goes on.

Our lives can be boiled down to a series of decisions, some major, some minor, some conscious, some unconscious, some that ultimately turn out to be the right ones and others that we live to regret. The bottom line is that, for better or for worse, we all know how to make decisions already. The question is: do we know how to make *good* decisions and do we know how to apply our considerable talents in decision-making to making good *ethical* decisions?

WHY MAKE A DECISION AT ALL?

What would happen if you chose not to make a decision in any given conundrum that might face you in your life? Which university should I choose? Oh, I can't decide, so I won't. Which job should I apply for? I can't decide, so I won't. Should I accept that marriage proposal? I can't decide, so I won't.

In the end, in each situation, it should be clear that choosing not to make a decision is actually making a decision and does not make the situation go away. It simply results in your inability to have any control whatsoever over the outcome. But make no mistake, you still have to live with the consequences.

In most instances, ethical or not, making a decision really results in the resolution of a problem or, as ethicists prefer to call it, a *dilemma*. A dilemma is actually a particular type of problem – one in which we are faced with two or more choices all of which are objectionable for one reason or another. If there were one clearly inoffensive choice beside other more offensive ones, then there would be no dilemma, no problem and no doubt about the right decision. Further, it would be a rare ethical dilemma to have to choose between a number of good outcomes. The bottom line still remains: a professional public relations practitioner has to be able to make decisions, and ethical decisions are among the specific genres.

THE BEST YOU CAN HOPE FOR

How can you ever know if you are even heading in the right direction when it comes to ethics? Short of relying entirely on your gut reaction – which is often referred to as intuition and is actually useful to some extent

– the type of decision that you are required to make in such cases is the key. What you need to accomplish is choosing a defensible solution.

An ethically defensible decision is one that you can live with and for which you are able to provide a reasonable, ethics-based rationale to observers. Make no mistake, you will often be required to provide such justification for these decisions since there are few black and white ethical situations about which everyone agrees. In solving ethical problems, it is a fact of life that there will be someone who will disagree with your decision. Where, then, do you find this defence for your decision?

There are several venues where we can look for such defences for our decisions:

- *The principled decision:* This is a decision which is based upon a well-thought-out application of the ethical principles that have guided ethical decision-making throughout history. These principles are those that we discussed earlier, such as doing no harm, an attempt to serve justice, telling the truth and so on, and the approaches to decision-making offered to us by such philosophers as Aristotle, Kant and Mill, to name but a few.
- *The precedent decision:* This type of decision uses a kind of case law if you like. Similar situations that have already been resolved can provide a certain amount of guidance largely because their outcomes are already known. This is especially useful since judging potential outcomes is clearly a big part of making ethical decisions. However, precise predictions of outcomes are usually not possible.
- *The patron decision:* This is a decision wherein we look to those who have more experience than we do in both our professional practice and in facing and dealing with ethical decisions. You need to be able to trust the judgement of your 'patron' and yet still be able to take full responsibility for the decision that you make based on such advice.

In the end, decision-making is a process – one that we know a lot about in our business, but one that has special considerations in ethical practice.

ETHICAL DILEMMAS: NOT ALL THE SAME

Not all ethical dilemmas are the same. In her book *Good Intentions Aside: A manager's guide to resolving ethical problems*, corporate ethics guru Laura Nash suggests that there are two types of problems in business ethics: *the acute dilemma* — when you truly do not know what is the right thing to do; and *the acute rationalization* – when you do know the right thing to do but fail to do it.[1]

Nash indicates in her discussion of these different kinds of problems that 'top managers often fail to achieve moral results, despite their good intentions, because they have thought only in terms of [acute dilemmas]',[2] the kinds of problems generally faced by these higher-level managers rather than those on lower levels of the hierarchy. Experienced managers have often faced similar situations before, worked through the issues and actually do know what they ought to be doing. Doing it, however, requires a different set of personal and professional characteristics. What often happens, however, when the managers who know what they ought to be doing fail to do it, is that they can be viewed by their subordinates as less than ethical, despite their clear awareness of what is right.

We can learn from this if we apply it to public relations situations.

An example of an acute dilemma in PR practice would be deciding where to draw the line between a news release that fails to disclose all the facts and one that tells all but might have negative consequences. These are the daily dilemmas that face PR practitioners all over the world. An example of an acute rationalization would be knowing that all the pertinent facts should be included in a news release because of their potential to prevent harm, but you hide those facts because you rationalize that members of the public who might be harmed have a responsibility to seek out such information on their own. What happens most often in public relations is that not just lower-level practitioners might see the upper-level manager as unethical, so too will the media and the public when the facts finally come to light, as they so often do.

DECISION STEPS

In public relations practice, we base our strategic approaches on a careful process which has four steps (see Figure 15.1):

- a *research* phase consisting of collecting all pertinent data, analysing it and determining the problems;
- a *planning* phase where one of the main tasks is to determine what we want to accomplish (objectives) and figure out the best way to accomplish it;
- an *implementation* phase where we carry out the strategies and tactics we figured out in the planning phase; and
- an *evaluation* phase where we figure out if our plan actually accomplished what we set out to do and more.

Making ethical decisions is a bit easier if we consider the phases that are similar to the above:

The process of PR decision-making revisited

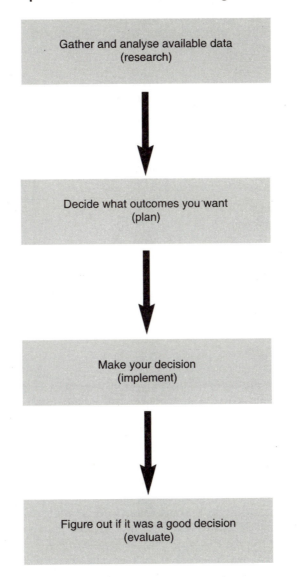

Figure 15.1   *The process of PR decision-making revisited*

- The research phase in ethical decision-making is similar to the data collection and analysis that we do in the PR planning process. The tricky part is recognizing that we are facing an ethical issue in the first place. Figure 15.2 suggests using the 'PR pillars' that we discussed in Chapter 2.

Recognizing an ethical issue using the 'PR pillars'

- Is there harm involved?
- Is there a missed opportunity to do something good?
- Could anyone be misled in any way?
- Will anyone's privacy be invaded?
- Is it unfair to anyone?
- Does it feel wrong?

Figure 15.2   *Recognizing an ethical issue using the 'PR pillars'*

Once you recognize that, indeed, an ethical issue is part of the situation that faces you, you need to gather as much information as possible about the following:

- how the situation developed in the first place;
- who are the involved parties on both sides of the situation;
- what current issues are affecting the situation.

- The planning phase in making ethical decisions forces us to examine the outcomes we want, but also to consider the outcomes that are likely, given the choices available. This is where we can use what has come to be known in ethics circles as 'The Potter Box' (Figure 15.3). This decision-making model was developed by Harvard divinity professor Ralph Potter and is now widely accepted as an organized approach to considering the application of values, principles and loyalties to making defensible ethical decisions (more about how to apply this approach a bit later).

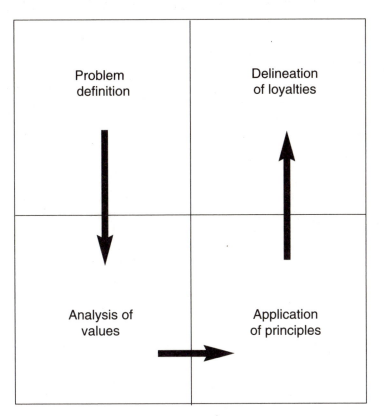

Figure 15.3   *The 'Potter Box'*

Once we know from our data collection and analysis that there is an ethical issue, we define it. The next step is to determine the values that we bring to bear on the situation. Then we apply selected principles to the situation and consider to whom we have duties. All of this should lead us to the next step in the process.

- The next step in making the decision is to actually make it, but this is where our ethical decision-making differs slightly from our PR process decisions. Rather than moving immediately to implementation, we move directly to a hypothetical version of the final phase. Implementation comes later.
- The final phase is to evaluate the decision to determine if it is a good one. This is where a second guess comes into play. But the second guess is accomplished before the first guess is carried through.

MAKING THOSE ETHICAL DECISIONS IN PR

Take another look at Figure 15.3, the illustration of what has come to be known in ethics circles as the 'Potter Box'. Potter first introduced this concept in his PhD dissertation at Harvard University in 1965 and then subsequently polished into this framework and published in 1972.[3]

It is based on the notion that ethical dilemmas result from conflicts that arise between any combination of the values we hold, the principles we use to make our decisions, and the duties we have to others. Here is how the Potter Box is used:

1. *Problem definition:* Just as in any kind of a decision that we have to make, the first step is to gather all available information that sheds light on how the situation developed and what it looks like now, so that we can truly pinpoint the problem. If we fail to define the problem accurately, we cannot expect to solve it to our or anyone else's satisfaction. It is analogous to a physician who focuses on a symptom rather than the true cause of a patient's problem. Dealing with the symptom still does not solve the problem. Thus, this is a very important first step in any attempt to make a decision about an ethical dilemma.

2. *Analysis of values:* Once you are aware of the facts of the situation as far as you can determine them, the next step is to examine your personal and professional values that are important in the situation. In general, values are those aspects of life you consider to be important to you and that guide your decisions about what is right and wrong. For example, if you value truth and fairness, these values are likely to find manifestation in the kind of decision you make about both your professional and personal lives and therefore will guide your behaviour. If you value money and the security you believe money can bring you more than you value the truth, this belief will guide your decisions. So, you have a full set of personal values; but these values change over time as you experience more of life. In addition, you as an individual hold a variety of values depending upon the role you are playing at any given time: parent, spouse, consumer, professional. Whereas your value system is likely to be fairly consistent throughout these roles, the relative priority of one value over another might be different in each role. (Keep in mind that not all values we hold are related to moral issues: a large number of them are amoral, ie without moral relevance. If you value punctuality, for example, this will manifest in how you approach deadlines. It is an important technical value to you but has no moral overtones.)

    In addition to these personal values, there are specific values that your profession – public relations – holds to be important in guiding your decision-making. Codes of ethics of most professional associations indicate the kinds of values that the profession holds. For example, the Public Relations Society of America has an explicit 'PRSA Statement of Professional Values' and indicates these to be the following:

- Advocacy
- Honesty
- Expertise
- Independence
- Loyalty
- Fairness.

The 'PR pillars' that we discussed in Chapter 2 are our values as we defined them.

Making ethical decisions, then, takes into consideration these values. As you examine an ethical dilemma at the stage of analysing values, you need to determine which of the values is brought to bear in the specific set of circumstances. If, however, you note that several of these are brought to bear, a priority value needs to be determined based on your professional judgement. Keep in mind also that when you are making an ethical decision in your professional life, best practice demands that you put your profession's values above your own. Indeed, the professional expects a practitioner's personal values to be congruent with the profession's values.

3. *Application of principles:* The next step in the decision-making process using the Potter Box as a guide is to apply appropriate principles to the situation. These principles, as they are interpreted by this model, are those approaches to moral decision-making that we examined in the first section of this book. For example, perhaps the situation demands that you use Aristotle's approach to finding the mean between two extremes. Or you might believe that you need to consider the greatest good to the greatest number of people. In the latter case, you would apply the principle of utility.

4. *Delineation of loyalties:* The final step before you make that final decision is to determine to whom you must be loyal in this situation. The four important loyalties are, of course, to your employer, your profession, society and yourself. According to most professional associations' codes of ethical behaviour, your most important loyalty in a given professional situation should be to your employer or client. Naturally, this is arguable. Whereas it is a good place to start your examination of your loyalties, there are times when your loyalty to the public will take precedence. For example, whistle-blowing is one of those situations where you have determined that there is potential

harm that could be done to society and therefore your loyalty to your employer needs to take second place to your loyalty to society.

Once you have completed examining the issues in the four quadrants of the box, you have enough information to make a decision that you can justify. Let's use a PR-related situation to apply this process.

A CASE IN POINT

Consider this case. You are a public relations officer for a large, research-based pharmaceutical company. Your company has a new drug to treat arthritis that is ready to be brought to market. Rather than marketing it in their usual fashion through their pharmaceutical sales representatives to physicians, they have decided to take a more PR approach, touting the great benefits of this new drug; although, from what you know about this drug and its competitors, it seems to you that it isn't any real advance, just a slight difference in chemical composition with the same effects as most other similar drugs on the market. Your boss tells you to design a media campaign that focuses on the great strides that are being made in treating arthritis and how this new drug is playing a part. Is there anything ethically wrong with going ahead with the campaign as planned? Could it harm anyone?

1. *The facts:* Arthritis is a debilitating chronic illness that affects millions of people worldwide; many of these sufferers are elderly, a vulnerable public if ever there was one. A new advance would be good for them. However, believing that this is a new advance when it isn't could be misleading. What has led to this proposed approach by your company is the level of competition in the marketplace and the need to position themselves in the minds of consumers as the best way to treat their condition. The proposed approach aims to circumvent physicians and go directly to consumers. From a public relations perspective, this could prove to be problematic in the future relationship with this important public.
2. *The values:* Clearly, honesty and fairness are important here, as is loyalty. If you use the PRSA's values as a guide here, this value of loyalty is one of being faithful to the client/employer while at the same time honouring an obligation to the public interest. In this case, honesty and loyalty seem to conflict unless you consider your loyalty to the greater good.
3. *The principles:* There are several principles that could be useful here. If you adhere to the categorical imperative to be honest, then your path is clear. However, for many in this situation, it is a matter of what is

likely to be of greater benefit to a greater number of people. If you go ahead with the campaign as planned, the good that will come will be primarily to the company and its investors. Will there be any good for the public? Not really, when you consider the harm it could do when the patients believe that they have been led to believe that this is the magic bullet they have been awaiting. In addition, there is no good here for the physicians who will have to prescribe this. Indeed, the approach could be construed as being disrespectful to them and could harm both them and your relationship with them in the long run.

4. *The loyalties:* Your loyalty to your employer is clear here: you should be doing whatever you can to maximize their profitability, but not at the expense of others. Indeed, other loyalties will not be served by this campaign either. If you consider your loyalty to your profession, clearly doing something that might reflect badly on it is unethical. Your loyalty to yourself is a bit more problematic. If you believe in honesty as a personal value, then your course is clear. However, if you value money more and you believe that if you do not do as you are asked you will lose your job, then your loyalty to yourself might suggest that you do something that you otherwise consider to be immoral. However, this is short-sighted. If you harm your reputation by behaving unethically in this situation when you know the right thing to do, the long-term ramifications for your career could be devastating, therefore showing considerable disloyalty to yourself.

Once you have analysed the problem in this way, your course of action should be clear. Just how you will implement the decision relies on your professional judgement.

OTHER APPROACHES

Before we move into the process of taking that second look at your decision, we need to recognize that there are other models for decision-making: the one we've just examined in some detail is not the only one. Another approach you might consider was developed originally for doctors, nurses and other health professionals who are faced with ethical decisions in their everyday practice. This technique suggests that we begin at the top and percolate our thoughts on a particular ethical problem through finer and finer considerations of the dilemma. The steps in the percolation approach to ethical decision-making as applied to public relations are the following:

1. Gather appropriate and correct information.
2. Differentiate between what needs we and others have relative to the situation versus what we merely want from it.
3. Examine relevant civil laws and codes of ethics.
4. Consider your moral duties.
5. Determine whether the proposed solution represents a benefit or burden and to whom.
6. Make a decision.
7. Re-examine the situation and the decision to determine if you need to filter any of the components further and from what point.[4]

Health professionals have been dealing with ethical dilemmas since Hippocrates and his famous oath. As PR practitioners, members of a relatively new professional discipline, we can learn from other more experienced professionals. Now we'll move on to that issue of taking a second look at a decision.

CRITERIA FOR SECOND GUESSING

The question is: Once you have made a decision, how can you test it to ensure that it is the right one before you implement it? What criteria might you use for a second guess?

The single most important test there is for you to know that you have made the right ethical decision is your unequivocal yes or no answer to one single question:

Would you be comfortable with this decision if it were spread across the front page of your leading national newspaper and your local media headlines tomorrow morning?

This is your never-fail litmus test, that crucial and revealing test in which there is one decisive factor. What if you can't answer an unequivocal 'yes' to this question? How can you figure out what's wrong with your decision?

In a chapter called 'Ethics Without the Sermon' in an old book called *Doing Ethics in Business*,[5] Laura Nash posed questions for examining the ethics of a business situation. She provides 12 such questions. Here are 10 questions derived from her original ones but that are especially pertinent in the field of public relations. These questions provide a basis for creating a series of tests for helping public relations practitioners on a practical level to determine when they've made the 'right' decision.

1. What is your intention in making this decision? Be honest about this. What exactly are you trying to achieve and for whom? Once you recognize what you are really trying to achieve, you may find that your decision really won't get you there.
2. How does this intention compare to the results that you can realistically expect from this decision? Most of us have heard the expression that 'the road to hell is paved with good intentions'. This is one of those situations when the best of intentions will lead you to the wrong decision if you are actively aware that what you intend is not the most likely outcome in reality.
3. To whom are you showing loyalty with this decision? Society? Your employer? Your profession? Or yourself? In the field of public relations we have duties to a variety of parties, but in these days of focus on social responsibility, our duty to society often needs to take precedence, although clearly professional associations stress your duty to your employer/client. Indeed, a high level of moral development and functioning demands that we take the broader view.
4. Will this decision harm anyone? The first rule of ethical decision-making is to do no harm. You need to consider all of the potential consequences for as many relevant parties as you can and take a long, hard look at the potential for injury.
5. Have you done everything possible to minimize harm? In the cold light of day-to-day business, it is not always possible to avoid harming everyone; however, it is essential that you take steps to minimize harm without rationalizing your actions.
6. Are you being honest in this decision? Are there elements of deception or subterfuge in your decision? Clearly, there is little room for dishonesty in our field.
7. What would happen if you were to discuss this decision with the affected parties in advance of implementing it? How might their input change the direction of your decision?
8. How would you feel about telling your mother what you have done? Your boss? Your peers? Your spouse? Your children?
9. Would you feel good about providing a salient ethics-based defence of your decision to anyone who questions you about it?
10. And finally, how would you feel about publicizing this decision to the world?

If your answers to any of the above questions make you feel squeamish, you probably need to reconsider your decision before you take action. This is key: second guessing yourself is done *before* you actually implement the decision. And the truth is that you often have little time in which to do this.

Finally, American management guru and professor Peter Drucker describes in his book *Management Challenges for the 21st Century* what he defines as the 'Mirror Test' (Figure 15.4).[6] This simple test of an ethical solution comes down to something very simple and very personal. Look in the mirror and ask yourself: what kind of person do you want to see?

Peter Drucker's 'mirror test'

Figure 15.4   *Peter Drucker's 'mirror test'*

Before we move on to a final discussion of public relations practitioners as ethical decision-makers, the following is a summary guide – a kind of checklist – that you can apply to making ethical decisions.

A model for ethics decisions: best practice in public relations

- ☐   Gather all pertinent information.
- ☐   Clearly define the problem.
- ☐   Identify the professional values.
- ☐   Apply principles of ethical decision-making.
- ☐   Analyse your loyalties.
- ☐   Make a decision.
- ☐   Second-guess your decision.
- ☐   Take action.

Figure 15.5   *A model for ethics decisions: best practice in public relations*

PR PRACTITIONERS AS ETHICAL DECISION-MAKERS

If you look around at your colleagues and peers you might wonder, given the way the media often paint PR practitioners, which of them is actually competent at making ethical decisions. And there is one aspect of your peers that you may not have considered when it comes to making such decisions. I'm talking about the issue of gender. Who can you trust more to make sound ethical decisions: a man or a woman? Perhaps you think that this is an unfair question, or that it is politically incorrect, but make no mistake about it, and feminism notwithstanding, we *are* different.

In a dramatic change from its early years when modern public relations was clearly dominated by the 'PR man', as a field of practice today, PR is increasingly dominated by women. If you don't believe that this is true and likely to continue, just call a few PR professors and ask them how many young men are in their classes. You may be shocked. Nevertheless, gender issues do play a part in PR, and ethics has its share of them. That's because men and women are not the same when it comes to making ethical decisions.

THE RESEARCHER TOLD US SO

You may have made some observations yourself over the years about the difference in the way women and men see certain situations and that they might even come up with different solutions to dilemmas. Whereas you may not be comfortable with attributing this to the gender issue, research has actually shown us that this is true.

In Chapter 7 we discussed the issue of moral development: that we are not born moral or immoral, rather that as we grow and develop our abilities to think, our abilities to make moral decisions evolve. We used the work of the late Harvard psychologist Lawrence Kohlberg as the basis for our discussion. He studied adolescent boys and their responses to ethical dilemmas and developed his theory of moral development based on the notion that whereas we begin our lives very self-centred, our moral abilities develop to include an ever-widening concern for others until we reach a point where we are able to use universal principles as a basis for our decisions. At that point we begin to consider the good of even those with whom we never come in contact – or at least some of us get to that point. In truth, few of us ever do, according to Kohlberg.

There was a lot to think about in this theory. It explains why some people make ethical decisions based only on what's in it for them, whereas others seem to be able to take themselves out of a situation and consider the right thing to do on its own. This just indicates a difference in levels of development. His theory was, however, based on the notion that rules and justice are what are most important in making ethical decisions.

Then along came a graduate student named Carol Gilligan, who became Kohlberg's research assistant in 1970. She would go on to develop her own theory of moral development, spurred largely by her criticism of his. She was concerned that he had gathered his data from privileged, white adolescent males and that the theory failed to consider the different ways that men and women perceive the world. Indeed, her own theory, described in detail in her book *In a Different Voice: Psychological theory and women's development*, suggests that we go through stages that are similar to those that men seem to navigate, but that women's orientation is different. Rather than being mainly concerned about rules and justice, women seem to base their moral decisions on a framework of relationships and caring.

It appears that males approach morality with the belief that individuals have certain basic rights, and that you have to respect the rights of others. Thus, morality imposes restrictions on what you can do and this provides the parameters for ethical decision-making. By contrast, the female approach to morality is that people have responsibilities towards others. So morality is an imperative to care for others. Using this as the basis for ethical decisions results in quite different ones from those suggested by males.

So, what does this mean to us in the business world of the 21st century? In these days of what appears to be institutionalized immorality in decisions affecting everything from the environment to investor relations, and where the highest levels of most businesses are dominated by men, the question is germane.

A study of the ethical decision-making patterns of public relations practitioners, done by a graduate student at Louisiana State University in 1998, also found that gender played a part in the decisions and that women scored higher in the questions related to 'integrity'.[7] This might sound immediately as if women are more ethical than are men. But the truth is they are just different.

The ethics research finds that men are factual and logical, where women tend towards more emotional decisions. Is this good or bad? Where men are rule-based, women are more compassionate. Where men are focused on what's going on in the here and now, women tend to be more focused on the future. Where men see things in black and white, women see them in shades of grey. Where men take a commanding role, women sometimes shy away from decision-making (the research with children showed that when boys are playing and have a conflict, they work to resolve it, while the girls stopped playing).

So, who is 'better' at ethical decision-making? It should be clear that there are advantages and disadvantages to each orientation. That said, Lois Boynton, of the University of North Carolina suggests that since our field of public relations has at its heart a focus on advocacy and helping organizations find mutual understanding between themselves and their publics, perhaps our ethical foundation is more clearly aligned with what Carol Gilligan refers to as the 'ethic of care'.[8] Her study, however, finally concludes that both this so-called 'ethic of care' as well as Kohlberg's focus on the 'ethic of justice' are legitimate bases for ethics in public relations practice. The bottom line is that there is much to learn from each of these orientations. In addition, there are other factors involved in making ethical decisions; gender just happens to be one of them.

We make decisions every day in public relations practice and in our personal lives; some are conscious, while others are automatic. Ethical decision-making is a skill that can be learnt, but it needs to be a conscious process at all times. The more conscious moral decisions you make, the better your judgement becomes.

In summary, we might consider Willem Landman's (the Director of the Ethics Institute of South Africa) suggestions about making ethical decisions:

● Choose values-driven actions.
● Choose right over wrong.
● Choose good over bad.
● Choose fair over unfair.[9]

Notes

1. Nash, Laura (1993) *Good Intentions Aside: A manager's guide to resolving ethical problems*, Harvard Business School Press, Boston, MA
2. Nash, Ibid, p 127
3. Potter, R (1972) The logic of moral argument, in *Toward a Discipline of Social Ethics*, ed P Deats, Boston University Press, Boston, MA
4. Parsons, Arthur and Parsons, Patricia (1992) *Health Care Ethics*, Wall and Emerson, Toronto
5. Jones, D (ed) (1982) *Doing Ethics in Business: New ventures in management development*, Oelgeschlager, Gunn and Hain, Cambridge, MA
6. Drucker, Peter (1999) *Management Challenges for the 21st Century*, Harperbusiness, New York
7. Lieber, P (2003) Ethics in public relations: gauging ethical decision-making patterns of public relations practitioners, Louisiana State University, Unpublished Master's thesis. Accessed 1 March 2004. http://etd02.lnx390.lsu.edu/docs/available/etd-0707 103-111615/unrestricted/Paul_Lieber_Thesis.pdf

8. Boynton, L (2006) Assessing the ethical motivations of public relations practitioners: adding the ethic of care, in *Proceedings of the 10th International Public Relations Research Conference*, ed M DiStaso, pp 48–58

9. Johnston, A (2003) Integrity: What this means for your organisation, speech delivered at PRISA Reputation Management Conference, 2003. Archived on website of the Global Alliance for Public Relations and Communication Management [accessed 2 March 2004]. http://www.globalpr.org/news/features/johnston-21-oct03.asp

16

PR and the corporate ethics programme

Aim above morality. Be not simply good; be good for something.

Henry David Thoreau

Social responsibility. It was the catch phrase of the 1990s, with ethics courses springing up all over MBA programmes, and organizational ethics coming under public scrutiny. It spawned a whole industry: the corporate ethics adviser. And public relations firms were right there to help companies communicate their new codes of conduct to employees and their external publics. In fact, ethics seems to have become something to be managed strategically as part of a public relations strategy.

The question that arises from this from a public relations ethics point of view is: When is ethics about the right thing to do and when is it about making an organization look good?

ORGANIZATIONAL ETHICS/PR ETHICS: NOT THE SAME THING

Before going any deeper into this quagmire, we need to clarify the difference between organizational ethics and its role in corporate social responsibility, and public relations ethics.

It has often been said, and increasingly so in recent years, that good ethics is good business. It certainly seems logical that ethical business practices are better than unethical ones when it comes to reputation and public image and enhancing the trust that oils the machinery of relationships between organizations and their publics. Thus, since public relations is in the reputation management and relationship-building business, there seems to be a clear relationship between PR and corporate ethics. What is less clear is whether some public relations practitioners believe that this is the same as ethical public relations practice. In my view, they are two different – albeit related – things.

Public relations ethics focuses on the ethical implications of the strategies and tactics that are applied to solve the public relations and communications problems of organizations. It refers specifically to the PR *function*. Indeed, Part 3 of this book focuses sharply on some of the most ethically problematic of these functions. It focuses on the ethical issues that emanate directly and sometimes indirectly from the strategic decisions that are made to meet public relations objectives.

Corporate ethics, on the other hand, is more broadly related to overall business practices and focuses on the ethical implications of the operational policies and practices of the business itself. While there is a relationship between public relations and corporate ethics, to imply that a public relations tactic that involves the institutionalization of ethics in a business is by definition an ethical public relations practice is a fallacy.

ETHICS AS WINDOW-DRESSING

One of the most problematic aspects of organizational ethics programmes and the public relations opportunities they present is the danger of making these ethics programmes nothing more than window-dressing where management pays lip service to ethics and PR capitalizes on it, spinning it into something it really isn't. And if you think that the ethics efforts of most organizations are becoming entrenched parts of their cultures, perhaps you should consider the results of recent studies.

The results of one recent American study suggest that 'the majority of Fortune 1000 firms have committed mainly to the low-cost, possibly symbolic, side of the effort'.[1] Whereas 98 per cent of the 254 firms that responded to the survey indicated that they have some kind of a formal document outlining ethical behaviour (presumably some kind of a code), only 51 per cent required any kind of annual indication of compliance by their employees. There was little evidence of follow-up. It is easy to draw the conclusion that ethics, for the 49 per cent of organizations that didn't seem to follow up their initial forays into ethics in any material way, can hardly be considered a part of the corporate culture and could be construed as nothing more than lip service – window-dressing.

An experienced, creative public relations department in an organization that develops a code of conduct and then does nothing with it would have little difficulty putting their strategic planning skills to use to develop a creative persuasion programme to promote the perception of a highly socially responsible organization – despite the lack of any real changes in organizational behaviour. Without these material changes in behaviour or any kind of adherence to the policy to support this image, what you have is an *unethical* public relations strategy. This specifically is when ethics is window-dressing.

Public relations is the most important external communication function in an organization and as such sits at the interface between the organization's decision-making and its external environment. The only way for public relations to play its appropriate role as keeper of the organizational conscience is for PR to be part of the policy-making team, representing the publics and their needs to management. Window-dressing is one of the most insidious aspects of old-style public relations.

SOCIAL RESPONSIBILITY DEFINED

Notwithstanding the previous discussion, there is no doubt that public relations can and should play a significant role in the social responsibility programmes within the organizations for which they advocate. But the term is so overused these days that it might be useful to go back to the actual fundamentals of the phrase.

Social responsibility provides a kind of ethical framework for achieving organizational goals. Planning for public relations programming requires both an understanding and an appreciation of the concept.

The organization *Business for Social Responsibility* provides a particularly descriptive definition of corporate social responsibility (CSR) as follows: corporate social responsibility means 'ensuring commercial success in ways that honor [sic] ethical values and respect people, communities and the environment'. They further elucidate this definition by indicating that CSR 'typically includes issues related to: business ethics, community investment, environment, governance, human rights, marketplace and workplace.'[2]

Social responsibility, then, means operating a business that meets or exceeds both the legal and ethical expectations that society has of that kind of industry. Note that this is a relative concept. What is considered to be socially responsible in one culture may not fulfil the criteria within a different culture. This is typical of ethical standards.

While it is clear that social responsibility underlies the ethical conduct of any kind of business, there are also other benefits that have been reported. Some of these benefits include reduced operating costs, increased sales and consumer loyalty, increased productivity, and an enhanced image and reputation. It is this last one where public relations practitioners most frequently see their role. Adopting ethical business practices and making a profit are certainly not mutually exclusive.

If a good social responsibility programme can have benefits for image and reputation, then it stands to reason that enhancing the ethical conduct of the business – and ensuring that the appropriate publics know about it – is a sound PR strategy. This in itself, however, does not ensure ethical public relations practice, the substance of this entire book. How, then, can professional public relations contribute materially to the social responsibility efforts of business?

THE CASE OF THE TRIPLE BOTTOM LINE

If we want to examine in greater detail the role that public relations can and should play in the area of organizational social responsibility, we should consider the concept of the so-called 'triple bottom line'. It is a business concept that begs for fuller involvement of the PR function.

The concept of organizational social responsibility was hardly a new thing in the mid-1990s when British business consultant John Elkington and his company SustainAbility coined the term 'triple bottom line', a concept that he later elaborated on in his book *Cannibals with Forks*.[3] The three parts to this business bottom line are identified as economic prosperity, environmental quality and social justice – where traditional financial bottom line reporting is augmented by reporting on efforts to protect the environment and to act in a socially responsible manner towards people.

Traditional accounting and year-end annual reports focus on the financial aspects of an organization only. Things like growth in revenue, return on investment, productivity and risk management among other things continue to be important to evaluating the relative success of a profit-making organization. The notion of the 3BL, as it is called, suggests that a successful organization also has responsibilities in relation to its commitment, and actions that have an impact on the environment and people – the latter including such considerations as health and safety issues, equity and equal opportunity, fair compensation and provision of educational opportunities for employees, among others. These are key components of an organization's reputation, and anything that helps to improve the organization's reputation is a key component of operational considerations in the public relations function. Thus, public relations' support of a 3BL approach to activity and annual reporting seems like an important addition to a strategic PR approach to reputation management.

There are few who would argue with the general notion that considerations of ecology and equity seem to be socially responsible complements to economic ones. However, whenever a new notion with a jazzy acronym comes along, there is an inherent danger. Before jumping onto the 3BL bandwagon as many of our well-known and highly regarded organizations have, you should consider how it could be viewed externally.

Writing in *Business Ethics Quarterly*, Wayne Norman and Chris MacDonald suggest that 'the concept of a Triple Bottom Line in fact turns out to be a "Good old-fashioned Single Bottom Line plus Vague Commitments to Social and Environmental Concerns"'.[4] They paint a picture of organizations first choosing their own data points with which to measure these concepts since there are few established benchmarks within most industries (few to none in the social justice category), then reporting on their accomplishments in, as the authors put it, 'a glossy 3BL report full of platitudinous text and soft-focus photos of happy people and colorful flora'. That glossy report sounds suspiciously like an output of the public relations department.

Clearly, there is a real danger that such programmes can become nothing more than very good examples of what we have previously called public relations window dressing without any real consideration of the outcomes for people and the planet. Such programmes, based on little more than good intentions, are ethically questionable in their sincerity and thus true honesty.

The idea of triple bottom line reporting is a nice one, and public relations certainly has a role to play in how an organization measures that bottom line. The most important consideration, however, is how those reports will be used and whether or not the actions are real or nothing more than smoke and mirrors.

ORGANIZATIONAL ETHICS AND PR

If we consider a number of traditional public relations functions within organizations, we can begin to develop a framework for understanding how ethical PR practice can also play a role in the overall socially responsible functioning of organizations. Here are some examples of what PR can do. These are suggested places to start rather than any exhaustive list of tactics:

- *Internal relations:* A sound PR strategy in internal relations can have a number of significant impacts on the ethical organization. First, PR can play a role in the initial development of the employee ethics programme. By using a collaborative approach and a belief in this public's right to participate in decisions that affect them, PR can co-ordinate employee participation in the development of an ethics code for the organization. This achieves employee relations objectives related to two-way communication between employees and management, enhancing employee morale, nurturing trust and educating employees about ethics itself. After the development of a programme, PR has a major role in developing a strategy to achieve employee buy-in.
- *Client/consumer relations:* Ensuring that communication strategies and vehicles adhere to the organizational code and that clients/consumers recognize that the organization's behaviour is guided by such a code is PR's major role. In addition, client/consumer relations programmes that emphasize mutual respect and a foundation of trust are part of PR's contribution to the organization's ethics programme.
- *Community relations:* This is a natural fit for public relations, contributing to the organization's social responsibility requirements. Strategic choice of donation and sponsorship opportunities, for example, can consider the real benefit to society rather than only the high-profile mileage that might be of benefit more to the organization than the community. Supporting employee volunteer efforts in the community is a way to enhance both community and employee relations.
- *Media relations:* Making commitments to media contacts about the level of ethical behaviour that they can expect from your organization might initially be met with scepticism, but eventually, when the promises are fulfilled over time, the relationship will be enhanced and the organization's responsibility to be truthful and transparent will be fulfilled.

Other areas of public relations such as investor relations and government relations (public affairs) are also opportunities for PR professionals to behave in an ethical manner and to contribute to their organization's social responsibility programme.

Before we leave this discussion of PR's role in the organizational ethics programme, we should consider the possibility that public relations might have another, rather less traditional role to play. That is supporting the role of *organizational ethics counsellor*.

In general, ethics counsellors have two overarching responsibilities: to help the organization clarify its values and ethical standards commitments, and to ensure that these standards are upheld by employees. As the keeper of the organization's image, it is your responsibility to ensure that the ethics programme does what it says it does, that the employees truly buy into the programme and that there are consequences for lapses. If there is no actual substance to this ethics programme (ie it truly *is* an example of window dressing), make no mistake, you will be the one who will have to deal with the negative publicity that could be the fallout.

In addition, the PR role as internal communicator can support the ethics officer's educational programming. You can help the ethics officer to determine the best way to reach employees and even to carry out the technical aspects of such things as employee orientation, ethics intranets, presentations and seminars, newsletters, and internal ethics blogs, to give but a few examples of the available tools.

Beyond tools, however, there has been a call for the public relations function to take on a more strategic role in ethics management and to actually play the part of organizational conscience. But *should* you take on the role of ethics counsellor yourself? The current wisdom is unclear on the answer to this question. A study supported by the International Association of Business Communicators supports the conclusion that its members are divided on this subject.[5] Communicators outside the United States reported even more reluctance to take on this role than did their US counterparts. However, the popular approach of making legal counsel the ethics officers of organizations can consign ethics considerations to fulfilling the letter of the law, a lower level of social responsibility as we have discussed previously.

What is perhaps more worrying, however, is that public relations professionals *are* often playing a role as ethics counsellors, a role for which many, if not most, are likely unprepared. This concern is based on the knowledge that most practitioners today have not even studied ethics and have little real background for giving such advice. This seriously compromises their credibility in this role. The most worrisome scenario however, is the PR counsellor who has no background but thinks that this doesn't matter.

I conducted a survey of ethics education in public relations and corporate communications educational programmes in Canada and discovered that while most people who actually study PR are exposed to a modicum of ethics that is imbedded in more general courses, the vast majority are never required to take a stand-alone course where they have the chance to really learn something specifically related to professional ethics in their field of practice.[6] My literature-based research on PR education in the United States revealed a similar situation (perhaps even worse since most PR students are 'majors' within other departments such as mass communication, journalism or business rather than taking a Bachelor of Public Relations or similar degree). Given the fact that a large proportion of practising public relations practitioners worldwide don't actually have an educational background in the specific field in any case, the problem is perhaps even larger.

Perhaps then, the question is not whether we *should* be taking on a counselling role as part of our responsibilities. It is the more fundamental question of whether or not public relations practitioners even have or could acquire the knowledge and understanding to make it one of their responsibilities. That discussion is the subject of our final chapter.

Organizational ethics and public relations ethics are two distinct areas of study and practice in business. However, if both are to be part of the organizational culture, both need to be viewed as inextricably intertwined. Then we can avoid the kind of empty promises that so many corporate ethics programmes seem still to be making.

Notes

1. Pennsylvania State University Press Release [accessed 26 June 2001] Many firms flagging on follow-up to ethics codes. www.psu.edu/ur/NEWS/news/ethics.html
2. Business for Social Responsibility [accessed 30 October 2003] Overview of corporate social responsibility. http://www.bsr. org/BSRResources/IssueBrief Detail.cfm?DocumentID=48809
3. Elkington, J (1997) *Cannibals with Forks: The triple bottom line of 21st century business sustainability*, Capstone Publishing, Oxford, UK
4. Norman, W and MacDonald, C (2004) Getting to the bottom of the 'triple bottom line', *Business Ethics Quarterly*, April, p 256
5. Bowen, S and Heath, R (2006) Under the microscope, *Communication World*, January–February, pp 34–36
6. Parsons, P (2004) The state of ethics education in Canada: preliminary study results, Ethics Network panel presentation, Canadian Public Relations Society annual meeting, June, Quebec City, PQ

17

Making business accountable: the 'new breed' of PR

Reading about ethics is about as likely to improve one's behavior [sic] as reading about sports is to make one into an athlete.

Mason Cooley

It has often been said recently that public relations, at the interface between the organization and its publics, is in the ideal position to take on the role of organizational conscience. This is despite the scepticism of many people outside PR. The truth is, however, that the extent to which this is a viable role for public relations is dependent on the future professionals in our field: that 'new breed' of PR. This consideration of future practitioners begs the question: can ethics be taught?

Teaching ethics to students (or practitioners) of public relations, or any other discipline for that matter, cannot provide any degree of assurance to their future employers and clients, or to the profession as a whole, that these individuals will behave in an ethical manner. Indeed, to provide ethics education with any semblance of a guarantee would be foolhardy if not downright unethical. So, why bother? And if reading is a part of continuing your education, do you suppose that by reading this book you are likely to take steps to improve your moral behaviour? I suppose more to the point is: do I, as the author of said book, expect you suddenly to become more moral?

BACK TO THE CLASSROOM

Ethics teachers have favourite tools and techniques for forcing students to think about their ethical principles and their own personal value systems. Put yourself in the following scenario. I know it seems to have nothing to do with PR, but we'll get to that.

You live in a large town with your spouse and two children, all of whom you love dearly. Your spouse becomes gravely ill with a terminal disease. There is, however, a cure for that disease. The problem is that it is the invention and possession of only one man – a man whom you despise.

You go to see this man who feels the same about you as you do about him. You tell him your spouse's plight and he promptly slams the door in your face. You begin to plot your next step. Would it be acceptable ethically for you to steal it from him?

If you have a personal, non-situation-dependent code against stealing (ie you tend towards the rule-ethics approach to ethical decision-making), then you would likely say no because to you stealing is always wrong and you would be duty-bound to avoid it, thus your spouse dies and that's the end of the story. But what if your children are dying? The whole town? Is it right to steal? Is it right to steal for what you consider to be a good reason? Can the ethical line over which you have chosen not to step be moved?

For those of you who are still right there, believing that at some point it is morally acceptable to steal, then let's move the scene forward. You plot to steal the cure, but when you arrive at the house in the middle of the night to do the deed, you are confronted by the owner. The only way now for you to obtain the cure is to kill him. Would it now be acceptable to kill him to save your spouse? If not, how about if both your spouse *and* your children were affected? The entire town? Is the morality of killing a matter of being able to justify it? This situation is actually attributed to Lawrence Kohlberg, who used it to elicit responses from subjects in his research on moral development that we discussed in Chapter 7.

What you have just done is taken a look at the extent to which your own principles and values might or might not be stretched. You have examined where you draw your own black line through that grey area of ethics and under what circumstances, if any, you are prepared to move it.

This is the kind of thing that ethics education can do for anyone, not just for public relations practitioners. The truth is, a person's personal values, whether related to lying, stealing, cheating or killing, or anything else, have a huge impact on their professional decision-making, whether in medicine, law, politics or public relations. If your values are so deep-seated, then, can ethics be taught?

The real question is not whether or not ethics can be *taught*, but if moral reasoning can be learnt. Teaching and learning are two different, albeit related, things.

TEACHING AND LEARNING

Teaching implies taking some kind of action to assist someone to learn something. Ask anyone who has graduated from an education degree programme and he or she will readily tell you that learning really means changing some kind of behaviour, whether that behaviour is the ability to solve math equations or make moral decisions. Thus, whereas we may be able to teach ethics or moral reasoning, unless something within the student changes, it clearly has not been learnt. Indeed, anyone charged with teaching ethics to PR students or practitioners must be careful to ensure that no one believes that the intended outcomes are ethical practitioners. There are no moral guarantees.

Authors Mary Ellen Waithe and David Ozar posed the following provocative question about the teaching of ethics: 'Does an ethicist bear some responsibility for the conceptions that others form of the effects on a student of having completed a course in professional ethics? We believe so?'[1]

Perhaps public relations faculties would have a different view of what they teach to their students about ethics if they were held accountable for the moral decisions made by their graduates. There is a significant difference between teaching ethics to general arts students – philosophy majors, for example – who simply have an interest in the subject and teaching ethical behaviour to students who will be expected to apply those concepts in real situations where there will be public scrutiny of their actions. Many ethicists have suggested that making morally defensible decisions is a part of the ethical burden of serving society (remember our code of ethics as a contract with society?).

Whereas most educators and practitioners alike believe that ethics should be taught to neophyte PR practitioners, as well as those with developing careers as continuing education, what is less clear is what kind of outcomes can be achieved. I believe that if we are able to motivate students to examine their own moral principles and values, and consider how these might have an impact on their decision-making, then we will at least have future practitioners who are morally aware and accountable for the decisions that they do make. But, I also believe that you can, indeed, teach old dogs new tricks.

Just as students can learn to identify when they are facing a moral dilemma and to examine their own ethics, so too can PR practitioners who have been working in the field for any length of time. For many current practitioners, there was no opportunity to learn about PR ethics in their basic education. The eclectic nature of the backgrounds of current practitioners is both a blessing and a burden. It is a blessing in that backgrounds in English, journalism and the social sciences bring a richness to a diverse field. The burden comes from the lack of socialization into a professional field, and ethics study is part of that socialization.

Ethics can be taught. The lingering question is: can ethics, or at the very least moral reasoning, be learnt? And if it can, what are your best learning tools?

LEARNING ABOUT ETHICS

As we near the conclusion of our discussion of everyday ethics in public relations, I offer some suggested ways that you might continue to learn about this often troubling part of what we do:

- Read as much as you can about ethics – in public relations, business, and in life. In Appendix 1, I provide you with a brief annotated list of books I suggest that you might consider adding to your bookshelf (and reading before you put them there). Whereas I, like Mason Cooley whom I quoted at the beginning of this chapter, tend to believe that reading about ethics is not likely in itself to make you more ethical, if you actually think about what you read and look for opportunities to put what you read into action, it just might help. At least you'll know the kinds of issues that are near and dear to the hearts of those writing about ethics today.
- Look for opportunities to take courses on business, media and public relations ethics. Even if you were fortunate enough to have taken a course while in college or university, you've changed since moving into your career. Take another one and take advantage of the opportunity to discuss the issues based on your new experiences.
- Sign up for ethics presentations whenever you attend conferences. Each person presenting about ethics will focus on a different aspect of professional ethics and will, no doubt, have a different perspective. Being exposed to varying perspectives can provide you with more ways of thinking about the ethical dilemmas you face every day.

- There are several popular movies that are likely to provide some food for thought. They will provoke you to consider the potential for abuse of power within the public relations and related industries. You might consider watching them with several colleagues, perhaps even as a professional development session for your staff. If you have seen any of them in the past, it would be worth your while to look at them again, this time through the frame of ethical issues within our field. I guarantee that you will get something out of them the second time around. One movie I recommend is *Wag the Dog*, a 1997 satire of the American political system starring Dustin Hoffman and Robert De Niro. The 2005 satirical comedy *Thank You for Smoking* will have you reconsidering the ethics of representing any client, any time.
- Watch the documentary *Toxic Sludge is Good for You: The public relations industry unspun* and consider why public relations ethics gets such a bad rap. It will be painfully clear.
- Write your own personal code of ethics and use it.

It is possible even for those of us who have been in this PR field for a long time to join the ranks of the 'new breed' of PR. It only requires us to reconsider our ethical orientation.

DRAWING TO A CONCLUSION

We have come a long way since we began our discussion about everyday ethics in the professional practice of public relations by examining our own level of personal integrity. We work in an industry that is so powerful that to practise in a way that is morally sound, we need to be ever more vigilant about what we do, how we do it and how it is perceived.

Ethics is fundamentally about personal conceptions of right and wrong and the willingness to apply our own concepts of right to real situations. Professional ethics, however, is more than that since it must encompass the personal ethics of its individual practitioners, but it both enfolds and transcends personal judgements to include accepted standards of behaviour. It isn't enough to use only your own personal value system to be considered ethical in the professional domain. If you doubt your own moral capabilities, when you are in a position to hire other team members, consider selecting someone who can take on the role of ethics watchdog.

Whether outsiders call us flacks, spin doctors or other equally pejorative labels, as professional communicators we know what our moral responsibilities are. Now it is up to each of us to find a way to fulfil those responsibilities.

Note

1. Waithe, M and Ozar, D (1990) The ethics of teaching ethics, *Hastings Center Report*, **20** (4), p 17

Appendix 1

For your bookshelf

The following are some books that I recommend you consider reading as you continue your professional development in the area of ethics.

Bivins, Thomas (2004) *Mixed Media: Moral distinctions in advertising, public relations and journalism*, Erlbaum, Mahwah, NJ

Thomas Bivins of the University of Oregon is a well-established public relations scholar whose work over the years has focused on ethics in our beleaguered field. In this book he provides well-informed discussions of many of the basic topics we've discussed in this book, with illustrative material drawn from advertising and journalism in addition to PR. The case studies that provide food for ethical thought are, however, almost all focused on journalism. So, if your work or personal interests run to journalism, then this book will be very valuable for you. Or, if you are just interested in understanding just how level the moral playing field is between PR and journalism, you'll enjoy reading this book – and learn from it at the same time.

Cohen, Randy (2002) *The Good, the Bad and the Difference: How to tell right from wrong in everyday situations*, Doubleday, New York

Randy Cohn is known as 'The Ethicist' in the *New York Times Magazine* with his syndicated column that is distributed throughout North America. This book is based on columns he has written in response to ethics questions submitted by puzzled readers and covers work life, family life and everything in between. You might not always agree with him (as I don't), but his answers will make you think about the ethics of your everyday life and your work in new and interesting ways.

Ewen, Stuart (1996) *PR! A social history of spin*, Basic Books, New York

Written by a journalism professor, this book is one of the most detailed histories of modern public relations that has ever been published. The author's obvious biases aside, the narrative begins with Ewen's interview with Edward Bernays near the end of his life and then takes a sociological view of the development of our field. This is a must-read for anyone who truly wants to know where we have come from. And knowing where we have come from can often provide a better understanding of where we ought to go.

Fitzpatrick, Kathy and Bronstein, Carolyn (2006) *Ethics in Public Relations: Responsible advocacy*, Sage, Thousand Oaks, CA

A veritable who's who of public relations scholars contributes to this collection of essays on a variety of topics that relate specifically to the field of public relations ethics. Its underlying theme revolves around the concept of how to be a responsible (ethical) advocate for an organization in the 'marketplace of ideas'. For example, Thomas Bivins (whose own book I've also recommended in this list) contributes an essay on 'Responsibility and advocacy', while Kirk Hallahan, another well-published scholar, provides one on 'Responsible online communication'.

Nash, Laura (1993) *Good Intentions Aside: A manager's guide to resolving ethical problems*, Harvard Business School Press, Boston, MA

Ethics scholar Laura Nash has a way of writing about business ethics that is at once refreshing and accessible. This book really makes the point that good ethics is good business today and provides a sound examination of the application of ethics principles in business situations of all kinds.

Nelson, Joyce (1989) *Sultans of Sleaze: Public relations and the media*, Between the Lines, Toronto

This is a classic. It is currently out of print, but if you can find a copy, it is well worth the read. Media critic Joyce Nelson paints a very sleazy picture of the public relations industry and how it manipulates the media and in turn the public. She examines the tactics that we use to 'manufacture consent' as Edward Bernays would have said. This one-sided picture of your field just might make you mad enough to do something about the perception of our ethics.

Robinson, Dave (author) and Garratt, Chris (illus) (1996) *Introducing Ethics*, Totem Books, New York

This small book is one of those illustrated volumes designed to simplify complex subjects for the rest of us, and I find this one particularly good. If you ever wanted to know how ethical thought developed from Socrates through Machiavelli and on to the present day, but don't want to read a dense volume about ethical theory, this overview is for you and might prompt you to delve further into ethics.

Seib, Philip and Fitzpatrick, Kathy (1995) *Public Relations Ethics*, Harcourt Brace College Publishers, London

I would be remiss if I did not recommend that you read this little volume devoted to public relations ethics. Public relations academics Seib and Fitzpatrick have provided one of the very few volumes on this specific subject and I have used this as a textbook in my ethics course. Whereas they don't cover a large number of specific ethics situations, one of the strengths of this book is its sense of an overview of the subject and their nice bibliography that might lead you to the periodical literature related to our subject.

Stauber, John and Rampton, Sheldon (1995) *Toxic Sludge is Good for You: Lies, damn lies and the public relations industry*, Common Courage Press, Monroe, ME

I can't stress enough how important it is for public relations practitioners to understand what is being written about their industry. This is how we can understand the scepticism that surrounds our field. And make no mistake, the behind-the-scenes descriptions of the unethical practices within our industry that Stauber and Rampton portray are well researched and compellingly presented, notwithstanding the clear bias of their presentations. This is a book that you should read and discuss with your colleagues. You might also consider reading their newer books *Trust Us, We're Experts!: How industry manipulates science and gambles with your future* and *Weapons of Mass Deception: The uses of propaganda in Bush's war on Iraq.*

Vogel, David (2006) *The Market for Virtue: The potential and limits of corporate social responsibility*, Brookings Institution Press, Washington, DC

All public relations practitioners who consider the corporate social responsibility programme in their organization to be at least a part of the public relations function (and everyone ought to) will find this a very useful book. The thesis of the book is as follows: 'There is a place in the market economy for responsible firms. But there is also a large place for their less responsible competitors' (p 3). By examining what it takes to be a 'virtuous' organization, the author examines for us both sides of the issue: what CSR can accomplish, and what it cannot. Vogel, a professor of business ethics at the University of California at Berkley, presents a very interesting case for the relationship between ethics and profits, which he supports by academic literature and real-life experiences. But don't be put off. His writing style is far from academic; *The Market for Virtue* is accessible and a good read. This would make a terrific book for your PR ethics book club discussion group.

Waluchow, Wilfrid (2003) *The Dimensions of Ethics: An introduction to ethical theory*, Broadview Press, Peterborough, ON

Sometimes it's very important to truly understand the underlying principles that govern ethical behaviour. The problem is that all too often the material available is written in a dense, relatively inaccessible way that makes the reader want to yawn rather than continue slogging. This is not one of those tomes. Written by a knowledgeable philosopher, this book is one of the best-written foundational books on ethical thought that I've ever read. The author has a real facility for making these theories both comprehensible and interesting. He includes a wide variety of illustrative examples, covering areas from relativism, divine command theory (which we did not discuss in this book in relation to professional ethics), utilitarianism, deontology, virtue ethics and feminist ethics.

Appendix 2

Chartered Institute of Public Relations Code of Conduct*

(Reproduced by permission of the CIPR)

Section A

CIPR Principles

1. Members of the Chartered Institute of Public Relations agree to:
    i. Maintain the highest standards of professional endeavour, integrity, confidentiality, financial propriety and personal conduct;
    ii. Deal honestly and fairly in business with employers, employees, clients, fellow professionals, other professions and the public;

---

*In our discussions of ethics in public relations practice and its application to best practice, we have referred from time to time to the codes of ethics of professional associations. For your reference and with their permission, I am providing here the relevant parts of the code of conduct of the Chartered Institute of Public Relations in the UK.

iii. Respect the customs, practices and codes of clients, employers, colleagues, fellow professionals and other professions in all countries where they practise;

iv. Take all reasonable care to ensure employment best practice including giving no cause for complaint of unfair discrimination on any grounds.

v. Work within the legal and regulatory frameworks affecting the practice of public relations in all countries where they practise;

vi. Encourage professional training and development among members of the profession.

vii. Respect and abide by this Code and related Notes of Guidance issued by the Institute of Public Relations and encourage others to do the same.

Principles of Good Practice

2. Fundamental to good public relations practice are:

Integrity

- Honest and responsible regard for the public interest;
- Checking the reliability and accuracy of information before dissemination;
- Never knowingly misleading clients, employers, employees, colleagues and fellow professionals about the nature of representation or what can be competently delivered and achieved;
- Supporting the CIPR Principles by bringing to the attention of the CIPR examples of malpractice and unprofessional conduct.

Competence

- Being aware of the limitations of professional competence: without limiting realistic scope for development, being willing to accept or delegate only that work for which practitioners are suitably skilled and experienced;
- Where appropriate, collaborating on projects to ensure the necessary skill base;
- Transparency and conflicts of interest;
- Disclosing to employers, clients or potential clients any financial interest in a supplier being recommended or engaged;
- Declaring conflicts of interest (or circumstances which may give rise to them) in writing to clients, potential clients and employers as soon as they arise:

- Ensuring that services provided are costed and accounted for in a manner that conforms to accepted business practice and ethics.

Confidentiality

- Safeguarding the confidences of present and former clients and employers;
- Being careful to avoid using confidential and 'insider' information to the disadvantage or prejudice of clients and employers, or to self-advantage of any kind;
- Not disclosing confidential information unless specific permission has been granted or the public interest is at stake or if required by law.

Maintaining professional standards

3. CIPR members are encouraged to spread awareness and pride in the public relations profession where practicable by, for example:

- Identifying and closing professional skills gaps through the Institute's Continuous Professional Development programme;
- Offering work experience to students interested in pursuing a career in public relations;
- Participating in the work of the Institute through the committee structure, special interest and voctional groups, training and networking events;
- Encouraging employees and colleagues to join and support the CIPR;
- Displaying the CIPR designatory letters on business stationery;
- Specifying a preference for CIPR applicants for staff positions advertised;
- Evaluating the practice of public relations through use of the CIPR Research & Evaluation Toolkit and other quality management and quality assurance systems (eg ISO standards); and constantly striving to improve the quality of business performance;
- Sharing information on good practice with members and, equally, referring perceived examples of poor practice to the Institute.

Appendix 3

Guidelines for the ethics audit

Introduction

Social responsibility audits have been around for some years. And since they are closely related to image, reputation and relationships between organizations and their publics, they have been of great interest to public relations practitioners. In general, social responsibility has been described as having three levels.

I. The first level involves *minimal legal compliance*.

II. The second level is what has been termed *enlightened self-interest*. This is often where PR comes in. The organization's good works are used as a strategic tool to position the organization in the marketplace as being superior to its competitors.

III. The highest level is representative of a kind of higher level of ethical thinking: the organization does good works because of a *belief in a responsibility to contribute to the community* regardless of payback to the organization's bottom line.

Ethics audits, while covering some of the same ground, are a bit different. Ethics audits also include an evaluation of the organization's specific ethics progamme, including their code of behaviour and the extent to which employees abide by it.

Just as there are three levels of social responsibility – and audits to cover each – there are several different levels of ethics auditing. According to Frank Navran,[1] writing online for the Ethics Resource Center, there are three kinds of ethics audits.

1. **Compliance audits** reflect a kind of basic level of ethical functioning that is congruent with the first level of social responsibility. An auditor would examine the extent to which the organization's ethics programme, both its policies and the way these policies are implemented, complies with all required laws and industry policies and norms.
2. A step up, the **cultural audit** is one that is actually quite familiar to use in public relations. It's really an examination of the organization's corporate culture in that it assesses how employees feel about the ethical standards of the organization in which they work, concluding with a cultural diagnosis.
3. The most comprehensive of all the audits is the systems audit, which includes both compliance and culture, and then takes a comprehensive look at the integration of ethics into the way the entire organization functions.

Components of the ethics audit

The components of an ethics audit are not a universally accepted standard. However, there are aspects of your organization that will be examined closely. The following are the core components of the ethics audit:

*   Your organizational mission, values and philosophy and an assessment of the extent to which these are a part of the everyday decision-making process at all levels and in all functions.
*   Your policies governing any ethically related issues from on-the-job dating to whistle-blowing (and any other issues discussed in the foregoing chapters) and the extent to which these are applied fairly and equitably.
*   The absence of policies on the above issues.
*   Your record of behaviour, both public and private, as assessed by both internal and external sources.
*   How ethical the leadership in your organization is, viewed by both internal and external publics.

- Ethics training and development within the organization: presence, absence, value.
- Input from discussions with management and non-management employees in assessing both ethical behaviour and perceptions of ethical behaviour.

Note

1. Navran, F, [accessed 27 April 2004] *Ethics Audits: You get what you pay for*. Ethics Resource Center web site. http://www.ethics.org/resources/article_detail.cfm?ID=19

Index

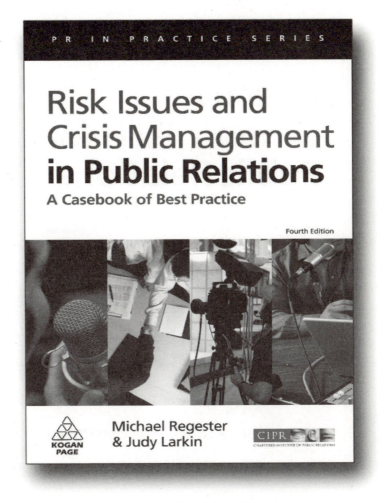

ALSO AVAILABLE FROM KOGAN PAGE

PR IN PRACTICE SERIES

Effective Writing Skills for **Public Relations**

Fourth Edition

John Foster

ISBN: 978 0 7494 5109 7   Paperback   2008

ALSO AVAILABLE FROM KOGAN PAGE

ISBN: 978 0 7494 5265 0   Paperback   2008

ALSO AVAILABLE FROM KOGAN PAGE

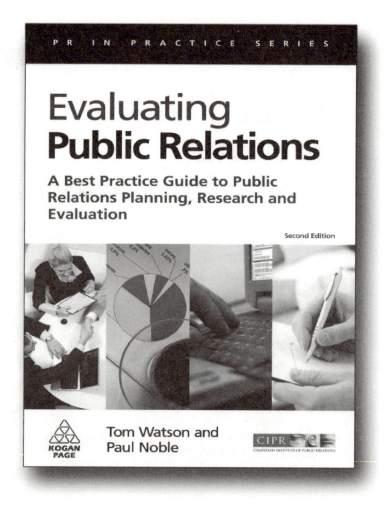

ISBN: 978 0 7494 4979 7   Paperback   2007

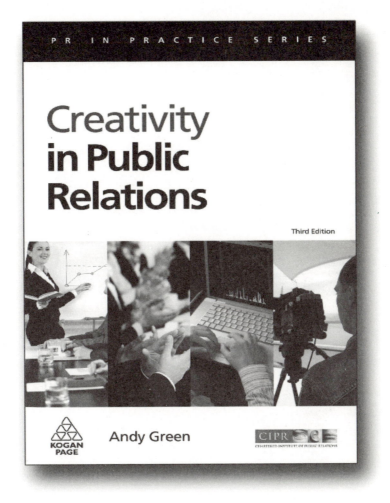